Georgina Muir Mackenzie

Notes on the South Slavonic Countries in Austria and Turkey in Europe

Containing historical and political information added to the substance of a

paper read at the meeting of the British Association at Bath, 1864

Georgina Muir Mackenzie

Notes on the South Slavonic Countries in Austria and Turkey in Europe
*Containing historical and political information added to the substance of a paper
read at the meeting of the British Association at Bath, 1864*

ISBN/EAN: 9783337310653

Printed in Europe, USA, Canada, Australia, Japan

Cover: Foto ©Andreas Hilbeck / pixelio.de

More available books at **www.hansebooks.com**

NOTES

ON THE

SOUTH SLAVONIC COUNTRIES IN AUSTRIA AND TURKEY IN EUROPE

CONTAINING

HISTORICAL AND POLITICAL INFORMATION ADDED TO THE
SUBSTANCE OF A PAPER READ AT THE MEETING OF
THE BRITISH ASSOCIATION AT BATH, 1864.

EDITED, WITH A PREFACE, BY

HUMPHRY SANDWITH, C.B., D.C.L.

AUTHOR OF 'THE SIEGE OF KARS,' ETC

WILLIAM BLACKWOOD AND SONS
EDINBURGH AND LONDON
MDCCCLXV

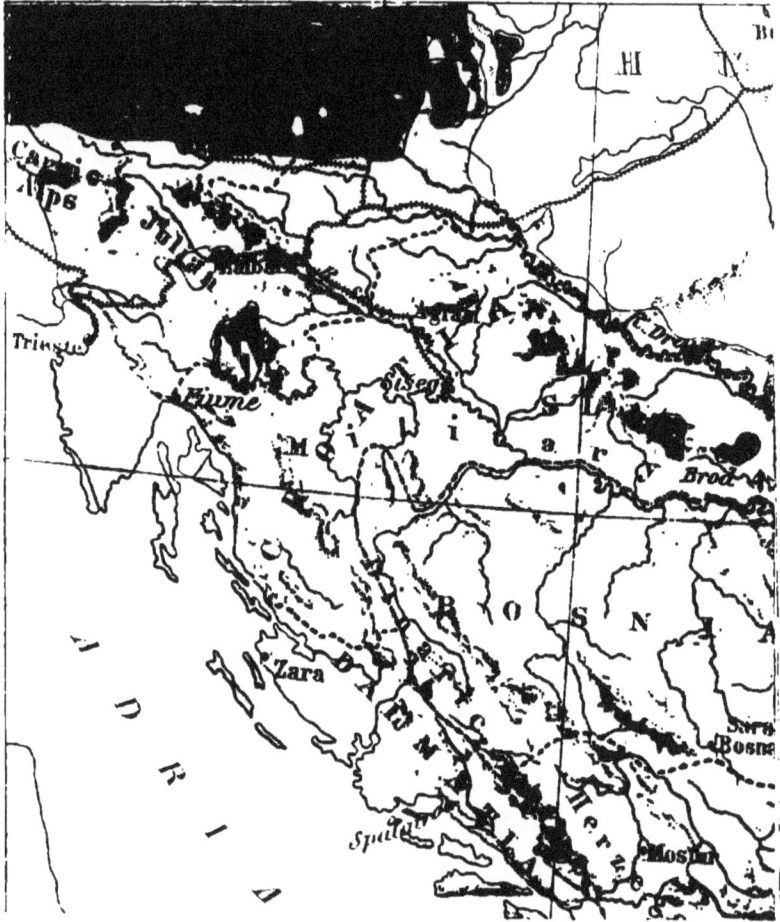

PREFACE.

During a tour on the Danube last year, I made the acquaintance of two English ladies, who had spent many months in learning the language of Serbia,* and in collecting information of the most valuable kind concerning that country and the neighbouring Slavonic provinces of Turkey and Austria. On my return to England, these ladies told me that they were preparing an account of their travels. They also showed me a paper containing notes such as would interest persons disposed to a practical study of the subject, besides answering several questions now afloat as to the nationality and disposition of the Slavonic peoples south of the Danube. They have done me the honour to ask me to edit this paper, adding to it some political remarks of my own; a request to which I gladly accede, in the hope that those interested in the condition of Turkey and her dependencies, may find in the following pages material that will be of use in forming a just appreciation of the state of the Danubian provinces of the Ottoman Empire, and in obtaining a clear view of British policy in south-eastern Europe.

. . . .

For some time past a gradual but decided change in public opinion concerning the Eastern question, has been evident in the speeches of our statesmen and the gossip of society. Nor is this to be wondered at. When, ten years ago, the nation stood forward to defend a weaker state from the aggression of a potentate whose arrogance had offended all Europe, we were in no mood to criticise the failings of our *protégé;* but, to make our cause still juster and stronger, we loved to imagine Turkey an inoffensive victim of that haughty Power which had crushed the

---

* Serbia—not Serria, the Greek form of the name, still used by our geographers, but given up by the French and Germans.

heroic Poles, trampled on the gallant Hungarians, and only sought a fresh victim to immolate.

The allied Powers interposed, and, at a cost of millions and of a river of blood, curbed the aggressive spirit of Russia; but when the question of peace was debated, and the war fever had cooled, we were reminded that some millions of Christians were living under the yoke of the Moslem Power we had been so zealously defending. We became aware that the Rayahs, or non-Mussulman subjects of Turkey, complained of a tyranny unheard of in Europe since the Middle Ages; that Christian evidence was not received in courts of justice, so that the Christian was in a manner outlawed, his life and his honour at the mercy of his Moslem neighbours, who lived as a superior caste among a disarmed and disfranchised people, whom the Mohammedan creed regarded as unworthy of just treatment. There were not wanting among us those who pointed out that, while resisting the encroachments of one tyrant, we had been supporting another, who, if less powerful, was more cruel and barbarous; that our sacrifices in behalf of the Turks had riveted the chains of fellow-Christians dwelling in what might truly be termed Egyptian bondage.

Not unmindful of this view of the question, our statesmen took care to exact from Turkey the most binding engagements to enfranchise her non-Mussulman subjects, to secure to them the right of recording their oaths in courts of justice, to abolish the odious "haratch" or tax by which they annually ransomed their lives, and to allow them the honour and influence attendant on sharing in military service as free men.

The readiness with which the Turks assented to all these propositions, the almost eager haste with which the Sultan issued the "hatti humayoon" in which he solemnly guaranteed the radical reform of the empire, tended to keep alive that feeling of goodwill towards the Ottoman which a close personal acquaintance during the war had somewhat endangered. If the suspicions of our astuter diplomatists were not allayed, at least they did not allow them to appear. The hatti humayoon was published 1856.

About the year 1860, Prince Gortchakoff, in a circular addressed to the European Powers, called their attention, in indignant language, to the injustice and oppression still inflicted on the Christian subjects of the Porte by Moslem authorities. England was represented at Constantinople by Sir H. Bulwer, a veteran diplomatist, who seems, however, to have forgotten, in this instance, the golden rule of Talleyrand, " surtout point de zèle;" for, as a checkmate to Gortchakoff's circular, he essayed to elicit the opinion of the British Consuls and Vice-Consuls on the state of Turkey, by a circular consisting of about twenty questions, which were accompanied by a covering despatch more than hinting that these same questions were to be answered in a manner favourable to the Turks.

The answers given under this official pressure have their full value. When the Consul reports favourably, we are apt to conclude that he is speaking *in terrorem;* when he reports unfavourably, we are forced to the conclusion that the state of the country must be bad indeed to induce him to risk official displeasure.

The sum total of the different Consular reports showed that Christian evidence was still, as a rule, not received in the courts of justice ; that Turkish judges were universally venal ; that neither life nor honour were safe beyond the capital; and that the country was, in most parts, in a state of anarchy not far short of what had been proved to exist in Syria.

The massacres of Jeddah, of the Lebanon, and of Damascus, followed by the combined testimony of numerous travellers, and by the publication of the Consular reports elicited by Sir H. Bulwer, gave a decided reaction to public opinion, and people began to suspect that the picturesque and solemn Turk was not altogether the brave and guileless creature that had been represented. This reaction was not arrested, to say the least, by certain speeches in Parliament and elsewhere in favour of the Turk and his loans, by the very persons who of all others in former times had held him up to reprobation as an irreclaimable barbarian.

Three years after the Syrian massacres, Europe was startled by the bombardment of Belgrade by the Turkish garrison stationed in its castle.

Several causes had led to this explosion. For some months previously the Turks had been engaged with the insurgent Christians of Herzegovina and the independent mountaineers of Montenegro, with whom the Serbs on the Danube, a people of the same race and speaking the same language, naturally and intensely sympathised. It is believed that several attempts were made to induce the Prince of Serbia to make common cause with the Montenegrines, and put himself at the head of a great Slavonian movement—a temptation which a prudent policy kept him from yielding to, as at that time the Turks would probably have had every assistance from England and Austria. As it was, the popular feeling of Serbia showed itself unmistakably towards the Turks at Belgrade, which city had become the home of numerous Christian refugees from the neighbouring provinces of Turkey. It is not to be wondered at, then, if the inflammable materials collected in Belgrade broke out in the form of a struggle between the two races. The Serbian Government foresaw the danger, and emphatically warned the Porte.* The bombardment originated in the murder of a Serbian boy by a Turkish soldier, who, on being seized by the Serbian police, was rescued by his comrades, killing the police and firing on the people. At once the city rose and captured, not without bloodshed, some fortified gates; and this feat was followed by the bombardment of a town full of women and children by the Turkish garrison without the usual warning.

The most obvious excuse or apology on behalf of the Turks is, that the bombardment was the result of panic caused by the menacing aspect of the Serbians; but the British Foreign Office, not content with this excuse, hazarded so audacious an apology for their *protégés* that we should almost suspect Earl Russell of perpetrating a grim joke had he not the character of being a grave man. It was actually suggested that the whole affair was a plot of the *Serbians* (not the Turks), that the Christians had provoked the bombardment in order to gain a diplomatic advantage. We can understand a people doing much to get rid of a foreign garrison, but that they should voluntarily expose their wives and children, as well as themselves, to the mercies of a soldiery who but two years before had proved at Damascus what they were capable of, is asking too much of our credulity. Had it been discovered that the women and children had left the city in any number, there might have been some colour for the supposition; but such was not the case, and even the Princess was dwelling under the guns of the fortress.

The British Consul-General on this occasion distinguished himself no less by the fearless energy with which he exposed his life in endeavouring to stay the fire, than by his indignant de-

* It is time we should cease misquoting the Prime Minister of Serbia to the effect that, until the return of the Obrenovitch princes, there had occurred only two instances of quarrel between Turks and Serbians. The Minister himself, and other Serbians in his name, have denied that such a statement ever was made, or could have been made. They have published this denial, and presented it to the British Houses of Parliament. The incident, if related at all, should be related thus:—"The Minister of Serbia, in conversation with the British Consul-General at Belgrade, expressed his conviction that if the Turks remained in the city an outbreak could not be avoided;" adding, "that while he had been in office, *before the return of the Obrenovitch princes*, there had been *already* TWO *occasions on which the bickerings between Turks and Serbians had nearly led to the gravest complications.*" The Consul-General being unable to converse with the Serbian Minister without the assistance of an interpreter, and imperfectly comprehending the statement as interpreted, reported to his Government that the Serbian Minister had told him that, previous to the return of the Obrenovitch princes, Turks and Serbians had only quarrelled twice. The misstatement was taken up and has been made the most of, while its repeated refutation by the Serbians has not been attended to.

nunciation of the cruel treachery of the Turks; until he received a rebuke from our Ambassador at Constantinople, ordering him to act more in accordance with British policy. On this, with the zeal proverbial in converts, he became an unnecessarily warm partisan of the Turks.

A writer in a late number of the 'Quarterly,' in commenting on this event, says:—"The precipitation of the Turkish commandant was punished by his immediate disgrace, and the Sultan expressed himself as 'horror-struck' at the occurrence." The *disgrace* consisted in the appointment of the Pasha to a valuable government in Asia Minor: no doubt the Sultan would express himself in any language that diplomacy dictated.

With the exception of Austria and England, all Europe denounced the bombardment, and the Serbs very naturally demanded that their country should now be freed once for all from the fortresses which Turkey kept up at great expense to herself, and which only served to irritate the surrounding inhabitants, and to check the development of commerce, while they are totally inefficient to prevent the invasion of the Ottoman Empire by a foreign power. A pretty diplomatic contest arose from the bombardment. It was found that the Turks had not even confined themselves within the fortresses to which they were limited by treaty; that they had lingered in the towns surrounding the fortresses, interpreting engagements liberally in their own favour, and annoying a peaceable and semi-independent people, who, since their liberation from the direct Turkish yoke, had made real advances in civilisation.

The bombardment offered the European Powers an opportunity of checking further Turkish encroachment. The contest in favour of the Serbs was carried on chiefly by France, Russia, and Italy, while the cause of the Turks was defended by Austria and England. These latter Powers succeeded in keeping the Turkish fortresses on the Danube, while consenting to the departure of the Turkish inhabitants who had remained in the cities contrary to treaty. Two small inland castles were razed. As for Belgrade, the lines of the fortress were again laid down by military engineers, and, to determine these with justice and *impartiality*, each Power was represented by a military officer to judge and decide between the Turks and Serbs. The British Foreign Office *sent Major Gordon, who was receiving £1000 a-year from the Sultan as inspector of prisons.*

During the diplomatic contest, the Prince of Serbia was beyond measure surprised and indignant that England, "the mother of free nations," should show such unjust partiality on behalf of the Turks, and that a nation of traders should do her best to retard the commercial development of his capital; so, setting aside official etiquette, he addressed a somewhat plaintive though dignified letter direct to Earl Russell, appealing to his feelings of justice. Bearing in mind that the Prince had before his eyes shells from a 12-inch mortar, which had fallen into his palace-yard, his language will not be deemed too strong when he says, " Can the Government of Her Majesty the Queen leave the country a prey to continual terror, at the mercy of the most simple accident, or even of pure chance?"

Informal as this direct correspondence was, one cannot but wish that it had been taken advantage of to inspire the Prince, and, through him, the Slavonic Christians of Turkey, with such confidence in the justice of England as would have predisposed them to be guided for the future by her counsels rather than by those of Russia. It is to be regretted that the noble Earl, in replying to the ruler of a small State placed in circumstances of trial and embarrassment, should have indulged in biting sarcasms, and then published the correspondence as something to be proud of.

For, after all, the discontent of the Serbs is less hard to understand than the policy towards them of our Foreign Office. They were told by the latter that they were practically independent, that they had perfect self-government and their autonomy guaranteed by the European Powers; the only conditions attached to this happiness were the acknowledgment of the suzerainty of the Sultan by the payment of an inconsiderable tribute, and the occupation of their fortresses by Turkish troops, more especially the large fortress of Belgrade.

The Serbs reply that the latter condition is insupportable, and no wonder. The inland fortresses, so long as they existed, retained in their neighbourhood a number of Moslems who, in defiance of treaties (which allowed no Moslem to dwell in Serbia out of the forts), lived in an irregular manner under the protection of the garrisons. It is asserted that these Mussulmans, no less than the soldiers themselves, annoyed the Serbs, by shooting their pigs and oxen, and plundering the country, always sure of a safe asylum within the range of the guns. Law was set at nought; for, even if caught, no Moslem could be judged by Christians. The Turkish fortresses are also refuges for evil-doers among the Serbians themselves, whether brigands, escaped criminals, or persons plotting against the Government.

At Belgrade a large Moslem population occupied one quarter of the town: many of them were respectable and useful citizens, many quite the reverse; but all, as Moslems, were equally obnoxious to a population that had lately been under their yoke.

It is a remarkable fact that those Christian nations who have at any time been conquered by Turkish arms, and who afterwards of themselves, or by the aid of others, have achieved a complete or partial independence, have ever made a condition that no Moslem citizen should in future abide in the country. In Hungary, Wallachia, Moldavia, and Greece, which have all at one time or other been overrun by the Turks, scarce a trace of a Moslem citizen is now to be found. The Danubian Principalities pay their regular tribute to the Sultan, and admit citizens from all other lands, but the Turk is proscribed.

These facts were taken into consideration at the Conference that assembled after the bombardment of Belgrade, in so far that, as I have already said, all Turks living beyond the walls of the Danubian fortresses were obliged to quit the country. Such being the case, the fortresses that remain do not at this moment protect a single Turkish subject, while they are far removed from the nearest point of Turkish territory ; * they are not wanted to guard from foreign invasion a country whose integrity is guaranteed by Europe, nor, if attacked, could they protect it for a moment against a Russian or Austrian force. Indeed, except Belgrade, which is kept up at an immense cost, at a time when Turkey is living on yearly loans, and borrowing to pay the interest of accumulating debt, these fortresses are but medieval strongholds, whose battlements would be likely to come down under the discharge of their own artillery. As for Belgrade, the only Power against which it can be supposed to guard is Austria, and Austria it is who positively demands its maintenance, and on whom, in cases of quarrel with the Serbians, it has depended, and must depend, for supplies.† Seeing, then, that these fortresses intensely annoy the Serbians, it is a fair question, For what object are they maintained ?

It is evident that a frontier guarded by a people jealous above all things to preserve their nationality, would oppose a great difficulty to an invasion of Austrians or Russians, of whom they are always jealous ;‡ while a people smarting from the constant

* During last spring, even Mohammedan Asiatic soldiers frequently deserted from the fortress and took refuge with the Serbs. Two of them certainly, and probably as many as seven, became Christians to escape being returned.

† The Serbs themselves are persuaded that the maintenance of Turkish fortresses amongst them is due to Austria, who insists on it, because they secure her, whenever she chooses, a *pied à terre* in Serbia, for Turkey can only defend them by her aid.

‡ The conduct of the Serbians during the Crimean war is one evidence of such sentiments. They refused Russia to side with her; but when they were asked to allow Turkish troops a passage through their territory, they refused that also with equal firmness; and on being threatened with an Austrian occupation, answered, " We remain neutral until the soldiers of any foreign Power

presence of menacing guns and Asiatic soldiers, ready to lay their capital in ashes, and manifestly checking all commercial prosperity, might in anger, and careless of the future, aid and invite a foreign army with the immediate view of ridding themselves of the intolerable evil. It is difficult to understand that, in face of such considerations, the base and origin of British policy in keeping up the fortress of Belgrade can really be, as the Foreign Office declares, a sort of sentimental regard for the " historic associations of the fortress with the ancient glory and victories of the Ottoman race."

It may fairly be presumed that, had not these fortresses been left among the Serbs, they would even, since the bombardment of their capital, have gone on peaceably developing their resources, and not troubling the repose of the Foreign Office, while their Prince would have been no less the vassal of the Sultan than the Prince of Roumania, who, within the last few months, has personally done homage at Constantinople. The fortresses have, however, kept at a red heat the most vindictive animosity between the two peoples. The British Consul reports, from time to time, the most horrible murders of poor inoffensive Turks, whose mangled bodies are found floating in the river, and draws a moral that the Turks are more sinned against than sinning. I would not exculpate these supposed Serbian murderers, but if I lived with my family in the neighbourhood of a Turkish fortress, I fear my children and household would lose their health from the confinement necessary for their safety; and if they broke bounds and anything happened, well, I hope I should bear it resignedly—but I might bear it no better than a Serb.

Since the accession of the present Prince, Serbia has shown a disposition to rely less on foreign Powers than on herself. In addition to a small regular army of 4000, the Prince has armed and organised 50,000 militia or yeomanry, with a reserve of 150,000. Shortly after the bombardment the Prince endeavoured to procure arms from Birmingham, but being prevented by the Foreign Office, he had recourse to Russia, and purchased there upwards of 150,000 muskets. These he had conveyed across Wallachia (in spite of the vehement protests of the British Consul-General) into Serbia, and having founded an arsenal at Kraguevatz, and engaged Belgian workmen, he had all these arms rifled and re-stocked, so that, instead of their old-fashioned Turkish guns, very apt to miss fire, and of various calibres, the Serbians have now about 200,000 excellent rifles. Last May I visited Kraguevatz, and to my astonishment found in this re-

set foot on our soil; whoever infringes our territory on any pretence soever, against that Power we will turn our arms."

mote place a formidable arsenal, with skilled workmen superintending powerful steam-engines for the boring and rifling of brass guns, besides all the appurtenances of field-pieces made on the spot. There were cannon, cast and rifled, of various calibres, from the small mountain-pieces carried on the back of a mule, to the formidable 12-pounder.

The ample resources of the country were laid under contribution. Charcoal in the midst of these forests is abundant, and the metals are dug from the neighbouring mountains, while the stocks of the rifles are made of walnut, only used in England for highly-finished fowling-pieces. I could not but reflect that British policy had called this arsenal into existence, and may be doing unintentionally a service to these people by teaching them to rely on themselves. Mere impatience of the Sultan's suzerainty would never have stirred an agricultural population to the exertions and sacrifices necessary for such warlike preparations ;* but it is more than enough to stir them if, after the experience of the bombardment of Belgrade, the safety of their dwellings and families is to be constantly endangered by the neighbourhood of Turkish soldiery.

. . . .

I have been considering the Principality of Serbia in its relation to the suzerain power, remarking that if freed, like the Danubian Principalities, from the actual presence of the Moslem, it is ready to acquiesce with cheerfulness in a state of semi-independence, which, in the mean time, secures to it the guarantee of the European Powers. But if we proceed to regard Serbia in her relation to the surrounding South Slavonic populations, we may excuse her if she looks forward to a day when, having become more civilised, richer, and more powerful, she may attract her neighbours, and form with them a united nation, with wide territories and respectable numbers.

It is surely not becoming in us to blame the ambition of the dependent or semi-independent Slavonians for desiring emancipation from the rule of Turkey, when our present Ambassador at the Sublime Porte has recorded the following opinion as to the characteristics of the Government to which he is accredited : —"Wherever," he says, "the Turk is sufficiently predominant to be implicitly obeyed, laziness, corruption, extravagance, and penury mark his rule ; and wherever he is too feeble to exert more than a doubtful and nominal authority, the system of

* In a letter to the House of Lords, the Serbians declare :—" Serbia is contented to remain under the suzerainty of the Porte, and to pay her tribute ; but she demands that her rivers, the highroads through her dominions, may be free, and that she may have full scope for the pursuit of happiness and civilisation."

government which prevails is that of the Arab robber and the lawless Highland chieftain."

I confess I should like to see England, in alliance with France, pursuing the policy so ably and with such prescience indicated by Guizot—a policy which, while defending Turkey from foreign aggression, aids and protects, rather than discourages, the foundation of new and immature states, which are gradually endeavouring to establish themselves on the visibly perishing rule of "the Arab robber and the lawless Highland chieftain." But, then, the question is asked, " What is to become of these Turks?" The question itself is proof enough of the universal conviction that Turkish rule is a condemned anachronism, and yet no better plan can be found than a bolstering-up of a Power which confessedly cannot stand of itself. What is this to lead to? How long is England to support "the sick man," and with what object? Let us support him against the ambition of his absorbing neighbours, but why be so inconsistent as to support him against his own subjects? We cannot for ever press down the aspirations and check the vitality of nations who feel that their opportunity has come ; and why incur the just hatred of those who, a generation hence, may have developed into a powerful nation?

The action of the Foreign Office for some years past in these regions has been at once irritating and feeble—i.e., has excited hatred without effectually accomplishing its end. It has been successfully defied, as in the instance just quoted, when the Prince of Serbia, publicly snubbed by the pen of Earl Russell, yet laughed at the protests of our Consuls, and introduced 200,000 stand of arms into the country. It was not of much use, after driving the Prince to arm his militia from Russian stores, to rate him in Parliament for so doing—after insulting the Serbians in their national sensibilities, to upbraid them for their Russian sympathies. Have they any reason to be enamoured of British policy?

Or can we expect them to respect a policy which indulges in inconsistencies like aiding the Turks to crush the Montenegrines, as we did by a loan three years ago ; or threatening the Italian sympathisers with our men-of-war when the Herzegovinians in their agony appealed to them for aid against the horrible tyranny of their Turkish taskmasters ; when, on the other hand, we all but aided these same Garibaldians in their expedition against a Government which, bad as it undoubtedly was, cannot well have been marked by characteristics worse than those assigned by Sir H. Bulwer to the rule of the Turk—laziness, corruption, extravagance, penury?

In an able chapter contributed by Lord Strangford to Lady Strangford's work, entitled, 'The Eastern Shores of the Adriatic,' his lordship seems to think that the future of Turkey in Europe is in the hands of the Bulgarians, who, as many believe, are an industrious, plodding, thick-headed race of dull peasants. He says of these people, " Neither Greek nor even Serbian has any right nor authority to set himself up and be trusted as their spokesman ; and they themselves have said nothing whatever upon the subject. It needs no inference from analogy, nor even the little direct evidence which we possess, to tell us that they are discontented with the details of the Turkish administration under which they live. But that they are disaffected and ripe for rebellion, or that they have yet risen to the conception of liberty at all, is not only unproved, but is exceedingly unlikely ; and the direct contrary is stated by Mr Paton, who can at least talk to them for himself in Turkish."

On this subject I may be entitled to be heard, having, like Mr Paton, conversed with these people in Turkish, which is in some sort the *lingua Franca* of these countries ; having spent some months in Bulgaria in 1854, and having again visited the country last year. When I was attached to the army of Omer Pasha in Bulgaria, I saw numerous villages absolutely deserted, the pigs running wild in the fields. The peasants had fled from their legitimate protectors to the enemy. During this campaign I sometimes ventured to sound the people on whom I was quartered as to their contentment and loyalty, and was amused at the cunning answers I received, and by the way in which discussions would be eluded by sullenly proffering some commonplace expressions of loyalty, such as " Padishah sagh ossoun," equivalent to " Long live the Sultan !" but anything approaching to conversation on their feelings and opinions was out of the question. I cannot think that Mr Paton could have extracted from them any more genuine expression of sentiment; for, unless otherwise known, an Englishman is always set down in these countries as an ally of the Turkish Government. Last year, however, I went amongst the Bulgarians with letters of introduction from their friends, and then I heard more than enough to convince me that they are ripe for any movement having a fair chance of success. Above all, I was furnished with abundant evidence of discontent, for some part of their complaints have found utterance in a Bulgarian newspaper, published first at Belgrade and then at Bucharest, and of which several columns are translated into French. Of these I was given files, and I choose quite at haphazard the termination of an article as an example of the rest :—

14

" Jusqu'à quand l'Europe laissera-t-elle se prolonger ce déplorable état de choses? jusqu'à quand fera-t-elle la sourde oreille à ces cris de désespoir poussés par cinq millions de Chrétiens qui gémissent sous l'oppression de la plus cruelle tyranie? Peut-être qu'elle n'est pas encore suffisamment convaincue de nos souffrances, pas assez édifiée sur nos misères; mais quand le sera-t-elle, si toutes les atrocités qui se commettent aujourd'hui ne lui paraissent suffisantes? Il y a de gens, nous le savons, qui doutent de l'exactitude des faits rapportés; et nous comprenons que devant de telles monstruosités on puisse douter en effet. Mais alors qu'on se rende à la prière des solliciteurs, qu'on envoie une commission faire une enquête sur les lieux mêmes; qu'on aille de village en village recueillir de la bouche même de ces pauvres et malheureux raïas les récits navrants des scènes mortifiantes qui déshonorent leurs familles—des exacteurs qui dévorent en un jour le fruit de six mois de travail—en un mot, des extorsions de toutes natures qui s'y commettent; et, comme en présence de la vérité le doute n'est plus permis, il faudra bien alors que l'Europe se déclare enfin convaincue, et qu'elle intercède auprès de la S. Porte pour que celle-ci veuille bien mettre fin à un état de choses qui déshonore son gouvernement en même temps qu'il est un sujet de ruine et d'affaiblissement pour son empire."

The details of Turkish cruelties as wreaked on these people I cannot transcribe, inasmuch as they are unfit for publication.

Some years ago there was a revolt in Bulgaria, and both before that revolt and since, any apparent apathy in the people may be naturally accounted for by the fact that Bulgaria, for the most part, is a plain interspersed with strong Turkish fortresses, consequently the last place to afford a hope of revolutionary success. The mountains of the Balkan, however, are full of patriotic brigands, genuine Robin Hoods, who make war on the Turks, and from time to time take signal vengeance on rich Christian usurers who are connected with their tyrants. These brigands are, of course, aided and sheltered by the peasants. I saw one who had fled over the frontier, and was lying by until his dangerous reputation had been somewhat forgotten, for the Turks had been roused to a hot pursuit of him. He was a rough-looking fellow, dressed in kilt and buskins, quite the type of a mountain hero. I met another far away from the scene of his exploits, in a European city north of the Danube, and he was a polished gentleman of vigorous frame, and spoke French fluently.

As to the relation of the Bulgarians to the *Greeks*, a most ignorant confusion has always existed in England on the subject

of the Christian races in Turkey in Europe. People have been
accustomed to divide the population of this country between
Turks and Greeks, including as Greeks not only the Hellenes, but
many of the Albanians, and all the Slavonians and Roumans.
The cause of this confusion is that the peoples of the East have
come to be designated by the name of their religion, instead of
by that of their nationality, as if all the Catholic nations of
Europe and a good many of our fellow-subjects were to be called
Romans. I trust that the paper which I have the honour of
introducing to the public may have the effect of, in some measure, clearing this confusion.

Lord Strangford truly remarks that "the Greek can neither
overcome the Bulgarian, nor lead him nor incorporate him."
Even in religion, which they have in common, the Bulgarians
are determined to have their own authorities. They are still
engaged in an obstinate contest with the Greek hierarchy
(Greek in blood as well as religion), and the penalty of excom-
munication hurled against them by a patriarch of Constantinople was unflinchingly endured.

This struggle between Christians has unfortunately furnished
one great argument to the defenders of the Ottoman power—
viz., that the tyranny complained of in Turkey proceeds from
Christian, not Turkish, authorities. To quote from Mr Layard,
"The documents showed that the real grievances of the Christians
did not arise from the Turks, but from their own bishops and
their own priests." Just so ; and by whom are these bishops
and priests imposed in Bulgaria on an unwilling people ? By
the Turkish authorities, who share in their plunder. This is
precisely one of the chief grievances of the Bulgarians, who
have again and again suffered martyrdom in their resistance to
these Fanariotes, who come furnished with Turkish firmans and
backed by Turkish bayonets. What does Mr Layard's assertion
mean ?—that England is to uphold Turkish oppression, because
Christians unworthy of the name are too often to be found
among its agents ?

The same Bulgarian newspaper which we have quoted already
furnishes us with a good example of the relations of the Greek
clergy and the Bulgarians. The following extract is from the
' Danubian Swan' of July 18, 1861:—

"Pour éviter de se trouver in présence de Mgneur. Dorothée,
le peuple avait fermé toutes les églises de Sophia et renoncé à
l'office divin ; mais S. E. le gouverneur a fait forcer les églises, et,
après avoir installé l'archevêque dans la métropole, il a envoyé
ses gendarmes parcourir la ville pour traîner de force les pais-
ibles habitants au pied des autels, et y recevoir la bénédiction de

Mgneur. Dorothée, qui déjà, dit-on, avait donné à pleines mains
sa première bénédiction au Pacha. S. E. a mis un certain
nombre des gendarmes sous les ordres du vénérable prélat ; les
uns devant veiller à la sureté de sa personne sacrée, les autres
parcourir la province et forcer les villageois à payer tribut à Son
Eminence Mgneur. le Métropolitain, lequel prétend avoir dé-
boursé sept cent mille piastres, somme qu'il veut à tout prix
rattrapper. Aux observations présentées à ce sujet à Monsieur
le gouverneur, celui-ci à répondu : que Mgneur. Dorothée ayant
fait de grands sacrifices pécuniers pour obtenir le poste d'archevêque, il fallait nécessairement lui payer ce qu'il demande
pour qu'il puisse rentrer dans ses fonds ; que du reste, s'il y a
des mécontents, il leur répète ce qu'il a dit déjà, c'est-à-dire, que
la S. Porte les invite á émigrer en Russie et à débarrasser le pays.
"Voilà notre situation actuelle. Voilà de quelle manière on
comprend en Turquie la liberté de conscience !"

The above extract needs no further comment, and is a fitting
illustration of those Parliamentary speeches in which it is con-
tended that the Christians, not the Turks, are the oppressors of
the people. Were it even so, what shall we say of the Government which has thus abdicated its functions, which allows
oppression and pillage to go on unpunished, and to be perpe-
trated in its name?

It has been asked, What have the Bulgarians in common with
the Serbs? The Bulgarians are, like the Serbs, Slavonic, and
speak a dialect of the same tongue. They differ from the Serbians in being more industrious, patient, and long-suffering, and
less warlike, though this latter quality, perhaps, only wants development by circumstances ; for, on the recent occasion of the
bombardment of Belgrade, a small corps of Bulgarians, headed
by Rakoffski, put themselves forward to defend the city, and
distinguished themselves by acts of valour. There are many
Bulgarians settled in Serbia, where they are esteemed by all, and
especially encouraged by the Prince, as industrious agricultur-
ists and good gardeners. Their differences of dialect certainly
oppose no practical obstacle to intercourse, and they and the
Serbs probably understand each other at least as well as a York-
shireman and a Londoner.

As for any future question of alliance between the peoples,
the Bulgarians claim to number from five to six millions, and
would certainly claim the fullest self-government consistent with
union under one ruler.* This the Serbs know, and are not of a

---

* Some years ago, when a change in the political conditions of the Ottoman
Empire was expected, the Bulgarians sent a deputation to Michael Obrenovitch,
present Prince of Serbia, asking him to accept the office of their ruler.

temper to dispute—indeed, they can never be in a position to
unite with the Bulgarians except by conciliating them ; and this
fact sufficiently assures the Bulgarian that he would hold a far
higher position in a South Slavonic union than he can ever hope
for under Ottoman sway.

Under Ottoman sway he at present endures what would drive
the most patient of people to despair. Of late years, numbers
of Mussulman Tartars emigrating from Russia have been quartered upon these much-enduring Christians, and been supplied
by them with food and lodging. During the past year I was
the indignant eyewitness of the quartering, amidst·these same
Bulgarians, of thousands of Circassians burning with religious
animosity against all Giaours, and ready for any mischief. These
Asiatics had been brought past the depopulated shores of Ana-
tolia, where their sparsely scattered co-religionists would gladly
have received them, to carry out the traditional policy of the
Porte, which here, as in Syria, sets tribe against tribe.

. . . .

I have digressed thus far on the subject of the Bulgarians to
show that, in antipathy to the yoke of Turkey, and in the desire
to govern themselves, they are at one with the Serbs.

To return to Serbia, whose position of quasi-independence
and the good use she has made of it are the hope and pride of
the surrounding Slavonic populations; it is generally allowed
that since the Serbs have been rid of direct Turkish rule, and
wherever they are beyond the range of Turkish fortresses, they
enjoy a degree of wellbeing that might be envied by richer and
more civilised communities. It would appear, however, that
some misapprehension exists as to their actual condition, at
least if one may judge from an article I read last year in the
'Morning Post,' which contained advice to this interesting
people given much in the style of certain Governmental
speeches in the House of Commons. "In her present state of
progress," remarked the editor, "at all events, Serbia's true
strength is in her great landed proprietors." Now it so happens that, throughout the length and breadth of the land, there
is not a single individual who can fairly be termed a *great*
landed proprietor. The laws of entail and primogeniture are
unknown. When a man dies, his land is equally divided
among his sons, the daughters being taken care of by a family
arrangement. When the land is too small to be thus divided,
those of the sons who are willing to emigrate to the towns
are bought off by those who retain the land. Thus there is
little or no chance of great estates accumulating from generation to generation.

B

On the other hand, the country being still thinly populated, and abounding in unreclaimed territory, there is no difficulty in any one obtaining as much land as he can cultivate, and in this manner allotments are made to immigrants from Turkey and Austria. Thus the country is peopled by peasant proprietors or yeomen ; and though, of course, their condition is subject to differences of wealth, and having few wants they are far from laborious, yet, on the whole, their wellbeing is remarkable, and nothing like pauperism is observable. During the whole course of my tour I never found a Serb a beggar ; the gypsies are incorrigible.in this respect here as elsewhere.

I found a remarkable equality in the condition of those of whom society is composed in Serbia ; and as education is diligently pushed forward, and every one is tolerably well off, no mob, in the true sense of the word, can be said to exist ; consequently there is no danger in suffrage all but universal, the conditions of a vote being only that the voter be a tax-payer and full thirty years of age.

I was also struck by the independent and manly courtesy of these simple peasant proprietors. On my entrance into a village the elders would come forward to meet me bare-headed ; they would then shake hands, and one or two of the notables would kiss me on the cheek. The children respectfully kissed my hand.

The oppression endured under the Turks causes the Serbians to hate the idea of a privileged class. Indeed their idea of such a class is what their fathers tell them of the Turkish Spahis, or what their neighbours tell them of the Bosniac Mussulmans, those renegade descendants of a Slavonic aristocracy ; while their notion of a "rich man" is the Christian usurer or farmer of taxes in Bulgaria, of whom observation teaches them to think it really harder for him to display patriotism, or disinterestedness, or pity, than for a camel to pass through the needle's eye. Hence, while it is an object of ambition in Serbia to make an "honest" appearance, and to entertain strangers bounteously, anything like luxury or ostentatious display is offensive, and considered as want of good taste. The Prince's establishment and his retinue in travelling are remarkable for simplicity ; and a rich citizen of Belgrade who lately built a house very much larger than his neighbours', felt so shy of living in it when finished, that he presented it to the country for an academy and museum.

In Serbia there exists a singular custom termed the Zadrooga, or family association, in which several families or branches of one family live together, having all things in common, and directed by elders under a house-father. The custom of forbidding girls to inherit land has its origin, it is said, in these zadroogas; for if they inherited, they would, on marrying, carry their portion into another family, thus spoiling the association. During the Turkish occupation the zadrooga prevented much misery, for a few roving Turks would bully or plunder a single family, but would hesitate to venture on a family club. The zadrooga is still favoured by law, inasmuch as it is necessary in order to have the land properly cultivated; for the Serb associates an idea of degradation with personal service, and hired labourers are with difficulty obtained; but these family compacts, acting like our co-operative associations in the manufacturing districts, make the want of hired labour unfelt. Each separate family is required by law to give a son to the conscription, but in a zadrooga two or three families are allowed to furnish but one man.

Another singular custom is that of " pobratimstvo "—the alliance of two individuals by mutual oaths to brotherhood, and co-operation in the affairs of life. Two men will thus, like David and Jonathan, swear to preserve an eternal friendship; or two women, in like manner, but sometimes a young man and woman—whose alliance, however, is strictly fraternal, rarely if ever eventuating in marriage. Indeed, I was told that a sort of horror is felt at the idea of a man marrying his " posestrima," inasmuch as she is his adopted sister.

It is a singular fact that Jews, so numerous in eastern Europe, are proscribed throughout Serbia, excepting in Belgrade. It appears that no sooner had the Serbs won for themselves the privilege of self-government than they expelled the Jews from the country. I was at first astonished at the apparently religious fanaticism displayed by this tyrannical edict, for the Serbians not only tolerate but subsidise both Roman Catholics and Protestants.* I found, however, that moral, not religious sentiments had dictated this expulsion. Wherever the Jew was to be found, he was a centre of demoralisation. He retailed spirits and lived by usury, and thus grew rich with the ruin of the agriculturist. The Jew was never an agriculturist, or even an artisan, but always either a money-lender or vendor of alcohol. The measure, then, deserves less criticism than at first appears, partaking more of the nature of the Maine Liquor Law than of the Spanish edict of Ferdinand and Isabella.†

* The Protestant Pastor at Belgrade has just published a German translation of Mr Denton's book on Serbia, together with notes of his own, thus furnishing a valuable contribution of accurate particulars respecting the country and people; he gives grateful testimony to the kindliness and liberality shown to the Protestant community.

† Another apparently intolerant law forbids foreigners to hold land in the Principality except on condition of becoming Serbian subjects. The reason for this restriction is, that the consular courts and jurisdiction necessary for the

But there are some things in Serbia that must not pass without criticism, and I cannot go the length of Mr Denton, in his interesting work on this country, in recommending the accommodation to tourists. That is to say, if you mean to be comfortable you must lodge in private houses, where you will always be hospitably received; or in the monasteries, where the accommodation is fair, and can be remunerated by an offering to the church-box. But the inns are still in the first stage of transition from Turkish barbarism to European civilisation. Instead of the bare walls of a Turkish khan you now find in every principal town an hotel—Heaven save the mark! In the smaller places the inns are kept by gypsies, and swarm with vermin, while the host is invariably extortionate. The roads are a wonderful improvement on Turkey, but, with few exceptions, are detestable to Englishmen.

Game is scarcely more plentiful now in Serbia than in Switzerland. The fauna of the country are much what are found in southern Austria; but a peasantry always armed, and who possess the land, have wellnigh exterminated the bears and wolves, numerous thirty years ago.

I would not be understood to praise, in an unqualified and indiscriminate manner, the institutions of Serbia. Though contrasting most favourably with those of Turkey wherever it is governed by Mohammedans, there is yet much to ameliorate. The people in the reign of the father of the present prince, the celebrated Milosh Obrenovitch, were accustomed to regard him as an absolute native pasha, and culprits would often, and not unsuccessfully, appeal to him to save them from the just condemnation of the law. Milosh was in truth a despot of powerful mind, but unlettered and unprincipled. His son, whose life is, morally and socially, singularly blameless, has incessantly aimed to teach his people that the law is supreme, and that even he cannot arrest its due course. He does not appear, however, sufficiently to understand that legislation itself may degenerate in the hands of bureaucrats, and become an instrument of tyranny.

When European law was introduced into Serbia to supersede that of the Koran, foreign codes were borrowed from wholesale, without due time and trouble being taken to weed them of their imperfections or to adapt them to the needs of a people in a primitive state of society. Hence much improvement is needed in Serbian

protection of Europeans in Mohammedan Turkey are still extended to Christian Serbia. So soon as these courts are done away with, the law requiring all those who hold land to become Serbian subjects will be abolished, but at present it is impossible to allow thousands of persons holding land in Serbia who were once Slavonic subjects of Austria, to remain amenable to no tribunal except that of the Austrian Consul. The continuance of the consular courts in Serbia is considered a great grievance, and applications have been made to have it removed.

law, especially in the procedure of the criminal courts ; and since
my return to England I have heard with satisfaction that the
National Assembly has authorised a thorough law-reform, and
appointed Commissioners to undertake the task. After much
and impartial inquiry, I have come to the conclusion that in
Serbia the judges are pure. I could never hear of bribery in a
court of justice.

After all, it is scarcely fair to compare these people, so recently
emancipated, with the highly-civilised nations of the West.
Rather let us compare them with those under whose suzerainty
they are, who are politically their superiors, whose ambassadors
represent them at the Courts of foreign Powers ; and having
so compared them, we may rejoice that they have advanced so
satisfactorily in the march of civilisation, while we lament that
in all essentials Turkey should have proved so immovable.

Lastly, I would not recommend, but rather deprecate, any
radical or sudden change in the mutual relations of the Serbian
Principality and the Ottoman Empire. If, indeed, all the Slavonic peoples south of the Danube should ever make out their
union in a monarchy, they will form a nation with numbers
and territory fully sufficient for a European State ; while that
stubborn tenacity of national existence, which, during centuries
of disunion and calamity, has preserved Croatia from being
absorbed by Austria, Serbia from being extinguished by Turkey,
Bulgaria from becoming Graecised, or Ragusa swallowed up by
Venice*—will cause them, as a united nation, to present a barrier
to Northern aggression far tougher than any that at present exists
in that part of the world. But in the mean time we have only
to deal with the little principality of Serbia, which, even were
her self-government extended to all the Serbian districts in
Turkey, would still be a small State in the midst of greedy
neighbours ; and unfortunately Europe is not sufficiently advanced in civilisation for a small State thus circumstanced to
stand alone, guaranteed only by right and justice. The possibility of being annexed by Russia, the real danger of being
knocked down and chained by Austria, present considerations
sufficiently strong to reconcile the cooler heads of the Serbian
community to a position of semi-independence. At the same
time, I assert, from personal observation, that Serbia, with her

* To save herself from Venice, which had obtained possession of the neighbouring cities, Ragusa long paid tribute to the Sultan, and voluntarily enrolled
herself as a dependency of the Ottoman Empire. This may be regarded as an
instance applicable to the present condition of the Serbians, who would will-
ingly guard against Russia and Austria by paying tribute to the Porte, if their
vassalage were divested of other onerous conditions.

resolute native Prince, her popular institutions, and her 50,000 men ready to march, is at once the nucleus and the mouthpiece of surrounding populations, all discontented and restless—all desirous to rid themselves of their present masters. And such being her position, I ask, is it wise to drive her to extremities, and to disgust her as much as possible with her vassalage, by showing her that its obnoxious conditions will never be removed unless by force? Or is it wise to drive her to seek help from Russia, by refusing her appeals to our own justice and influence? Say what we will in justification of the Turks keeping up the Danubian fortresses, it cannot be denied that since the bombardment their presence has been the incentive and the excuse for warlike preparations in Serbia. We are incessantly lecturing the Serbs on the desirableness of cultivating peaceful dispositions and commercial prosperity. Should we, in the case of any other people, ignore that the greatest hindrance to peaceful dispositions is the irritating presence of an enemy, or that commercial enterprise is checked by the exposure of the chief outlets of the country to an enemy's fire? France, like ourselves, gives peaceful counsels to the Serbs, but she proves her sincerity by at the same time urging the Porte to remove the cause of dispute. Mr Gladstone truly remarks "that immense advantage would result from a mutual confidence and co-operation between France and England in the conduct of Eastern policy."* No doubt the Turk would as heretofore allege sentimental regrets at giving up the Castle of Belgrade, dear to him as a monument of victorious encroachment on Christendom. But is it for Christian Europe to be tender of such trophies, or has Turkey, in her present state of financial embarrassment, a right to indulge in such costly pieces of sentiment? Without attempting to provide for an incalculable future, surely it is self-evident that at present the Sultan's interest is to live on good terms with his great Danubian vassals. In the words of Prince Michael Obrenovitch, lately addressed to his National Assembly, "Serbia, confident and contented, would prove a bulwark for the northern frontier of the Ottoman Empire far stronger than those wretched fortresses, of which the presence affords at every moment fresh cause of dispute."†

H. S.

* See Mr Gladstone's speech in the debate on Turkey in the House of Commons, May 29, 1863; published, with remarks, by Ph. Christitch, Serbian senator.

† While this was in the press, a letter from Belgrade informs me that soldiers from the fortress have broken into the houses of certain citizens, and attempted to ill-treat the wives and daughters of their inmates.

INTRODUCTORY NOTICE.

THE following Notes were taken during journeys in 1861-62-63-64, and appear in their present shape at the desire of persons who consider that, while the South Slavonic countries are daily increasing in importance, there are few parts of the world respecting which so little is generally known. Such information as we had opportunity to collect we therefore offer, but with great diffidence, and conscious that it can neither be complete nor free from inaccuracies, inasmuch as it is still hard to arrive at facts, especially statistics, in the Slavonic districts of Turkey. It is, perhaps, as well to observe that the name *South Slavonic* is not arbitrarily bestowed by outsiders, nor put forward by any Government, but was invented by the Croatians at a time when the Slavonic peoples in the south of Austria and in Turkey, having made some efforts towards a common literary language, were accused of *pan-*Slavonic tendencies. Need was then felt of some designation which would express a sense of kindred amongst themselves, and of distinction from the Russians and other Slavs. The' name "Illyrian" was first tried, but fulfilled its purpose imperfectly, because its Latin associations rendered it distasteful to the Bulgarians and Serbs. The name "South Slavonians" (Slav. *Iugo Slavi*, from *iug*, south) has answered better, being a mere geographical designation, obnoxious neither to national nor religious jealousies. Hence this term is every day gaining ground, and is beginning to represent a political as well as a literary idea ; although the Government of Serbia, fearful of representations from Turkey or Austria, as yet continues to disappoint the more impatient spirits by refusing to *afficher* any name but that of *Serb*. We frequently asked persons in different parts of the country what peoples they understood to be comprehended under the name " Iugo Slavi." One person thus questioned was an old Slavonic Mussulman, Bey of Bosnia. He answered by first enumerating all nations that speak Slavic, whose numbers he proudly exaggerated to a hundred millions; then he distinguished from the rest the Slavonic populations *south of the Danube*, classing them thus :—1st, Bulgarians, whose language differs from, but is akin to, that of the rest ; 2d, Croatians, Slavonians, Dalmatians, Montenegrines, Herzegovinians, Serbians, Bosniaks, all speaking what he called the *Bosnian* tongue.

THE SOUTH SLAVONIC COUNTRIES IN AUSTRIA
AND TURKEY IN EUROPE.

—

THE countries of which it is proposed to treat in this paper are as yet almost as little known to Englishmen as the interior of Tartary or the centre of Africa. Yet they lie within a few days' journey from London, and are connected with British interests by many and important ties.

In the first place, several of these countries are politically under British guarantee, and in case one of the insurrections of their Christian inhabitants should receive assistance from other European Powers, England might find herself involved in war to uphold her protégé the Turk.

Secondly, A district of these countries forms one of the most promising of the new cotton fields.

Thirdly, Through these countries runs the line between Belgrade and Thessalonica—a line which, if ever traversed by railway, will prove our shortest route to Alexandria, and considerably abridge the postal distance between India and London.

On these considerations we beg to submit to those who may be interested on the subject the following notes taken during a series of journeys through the South Slavonic lands.

Bounded on the north by the rivers Danube and Drave ;* on the west by the Adriatic ; on the east by the Black Sea ; and on the south by the frontiers of ancient Greece,†—lies a region not

* See 'Fröhlich's Ethnographical Maps of the Austrian Empire.' Slavonic districts extend beyond the Drave ; but that river, from the town of Villach to the point where it joins the Danube below Essek, may be said to part the mass of the South Slavonic population from that of the German and Magyar. From Villach southward to the Adriatic, there is no river boundary, and the neighbour of the Slav is the Lombardo-Venetian.

† The line of the Roman Via Egnatia, in that part of it which runs between Salonica and Ochrida, may be taken as a rough ethnographical boundary, though it leaves some Bulgarian country to the south, and some Greek settlements to

one-third smaller than France : its inhabitants, numbering from ten to twelve millions,* form the southern division of the Slavonic race.† Throughout the greater part of the country this population is homogeneous ; but to the south and east it dwells interspersed with about half a million Albanians, and some hundred thousands of Turks, Tartars, Greeks, and Tzinzars.‡

Classed according to their dialects of one language, the Southern Slavs may be divided into two nearly equal parts. The eastern call themselves Bulgarians, the western Croato-Serbs.§ Classed according to their creeds (we give the result of such imperfect statistics as exist), from two to three millions are Romanists, seven hundred and eighty thousand Mussulmans, and all the rest belong to the Slavonic branch of the Eastern Church.

Their political divisions are various. The Bulgarians live directly subject to Mohammedan officials, and their land is meted out in Turkish pashaliks. Of the Serbo-Croats, some are included in the Austrian, some in the Ottoman empire, and two small states govern themselves. Thus, we have the Dalmatians, Slavonians, and Croats proper, forming what is called a *triune kingdom*, whose king is the Emperor of Austria ; we have the Bosniacs and Herzegovinians, whose countries are Turkish provinces ; the Serbs of the autonomous principality of Serbia ;‖ the Serbs of independent Montenegro. To explain how these political divisions arose, and to give some idea of the present

the north. It would be more difficult to draw a south-eastern boundary from the coast of the Black Sea to the Gulf of Salonica, for the Slavs do not at any point touch the Bosphorus or the Sea of Marmora. In Thrace, Adrianople may be taken as a boundary city for the Bulgarians.

* SOUTHERN SLAVS.

1. In Turkey —
   Bulgarians, variously stated from   4,000,000 to 6,000,000
   Croato-Serbs, ... 2,633,000
2. In Austria—
   Croato-Serbs, ... 2,757,602
   Slovenes, ... 1,171,954
   Bulgarians, ... 22,987

† Or, as they call themselves, Iugo (south) Slavi— Francisé, Iougo Slave. See 'Revue des Deux Mondes,' May 15, 1864.

‡ Roumans south of the Danube, called "Tzinzars" from some peculiarity in their pronunciation. Their language in most respects resembles that of the Roumans in Wallachia and Moldavia.

§ Distinct from both are the Slovenes, inhabiting Carinthia, Carniola, &c. They claim to be among the oldest Slavonic settlers in this part of the world, and are at present anxious to revive their language, and to identify themselves with the South Slavonic peoples ; but, unlike Croatia, their country has no autonomous administration, and has long been incorporated among the hereditary dominions of the House of Hapsburg, so that it would be difficult to give particulars concerning them without entering into the wide question of the Austrian Slavs.

‖ Serbia— *German*, Serbien ; *French*, La Serbie. The Greeks pronounce the *b* as *v*, Servia.

position and capabilities of the Southern Slavs, it may be necessary to say a few words on their history and national characteristics.

I. We begin with Bulgaria, as that portion of the Iugo Slavic countries which is supposed to have received a Slavonic population sooner than its neighbours, though how soon is still matter of discussion.

Byzantine historians mention Slavonic settlers in the country now called Bulgaria as early as the end of the fifth and beginning of the sixth century. Several noted personages in the Eastern empire are referred to them for parentage—for instance, the birthplace of the Emperor Justinian was, and still is, a Slavonic village; the great Belisarius is said to have been the Slavonic Velisar; Basil the Macedonian, and his line, were Slavs. It would appear that the first colonists established themselves to the south of the Danube gradually, and recognised the Imperial rule; but in the seventh century they were joined by tribes of a more warlike character, under whose leadership they rose against Byzance, and overran the greater part of the peninsula. Who these new-comers were is still an unsettled question. Some Bulgarians insist that they were brother Slavons emigrating from beyond the Volga; but most authorities declare them *Tatars*, who, on adoption of Christianity, amalgamated with the Slavs. This much is certain, that from them dates the name of Bulgaria and the first dynasty of her sovereigns. Though often at war with the Byzantine Empire, the Bulgarians profited by its neighbourhood so far as to imbibe a certain amount of civilisation.* In the ninth century they fought covered with steel armour; their discipline astonished the veterans of the Empire, and they possessed all the military engines then known. Their kings and czars encouraged literature, and were sometimes themselves authors. As almost all accounts of them come from Byzantine sources, there can be little doubt that this portrait is not flattered. Under their more powerful rulers the Bulgarians threatened Constantinople: under the weaker they acknowledged the Byzantine Emperor as suzerain, and more than once Byzantine armies effected a temporary subjection of their land; but their monarchy was not finally overthrown till the end of the fourteenth century, when they were conquered by the Turks. Coins of Bulgaria are to be seen in the Museum of Belgrade, and a curious Chronicle of Czar Asen has lately been published in modern Bulgarian.

The most important incident in the history of the Bulgarians, is the translation of the Scriptures into their tongue by the Thes-

* See Shafarik, Hilferding, and Finlay.

salonican brothers, Cyril and Methodius. To this circumstance the written language of Bulgaria in the ninth century owes the position which it at this moment occupies as the ecclesiastical medium of the whole Slavonic race. We may here remark that the work of Cyril and Methodius is dated 855, and earlier than this it is uncertain whether the Slavonic was a written language. Authorities have, however, presumed that it was so—1st, because its state of development at the time of Cyril is shown by the fact that he was able to make an unusually literal translation of great part of the Scriptures, and to render the finer shades of meaning in the Greek original by Slavonic equivalents: 2d, because the alphabet with which some of the earliest Slavonic manuscripts are written, bears traces of a descent from times prior to the introduction of Christianity, and would seem to have been first cut on sticks after the Runic fashion.* This alphabet bears the name of Glagolitic, from its letter Glagol,† signifying "word." Glagolitic MSS. written in Bulgaria display a rounded character ; those of Croatia are more squared.

The so-called *Cyrillic* alphabet is supposed to have been introduced by St Cyril or one of his pupils, as more easy for copyists to transcribe, and readers to acquire, than the ancient character : almost all its letters are borrowed from the Greek, but a few are modified from the Glagolitic to express such sounds as Greek and Slavonic have not in common. The Cyrillic alphabet is adopted by all the Slavonic nations belonging to the Greek Church, but the Serbs, who desire to make their spelling purely phonetic, have begun to disuse some of its characters. The Roman alphabet, with accents to express peculiar Slavonic sounds, is accepted by Slavonic nations belonging to the Latin Church.‡ In Croatia all three alphabets are in use : the Glagolitic in church books of the Slavonic ritual; the Latin for general purposes ; and the Cyrillic taught in schools in order that the Croats may be able to share the literature of their kinsfolk of the Eastern Church.

To return to the history of Bulgaria. The last king, Shishman, became a Turkish prisoner in 1390 ; but the people submitted only by degrees, and on condition that if they paid the

---

* A curious little Reading-Book has lately been published, giving specimens of various kinds of Glagolitic writing. A collection of Glagolitic MSS. may be seen at Agram, in the library of M. Kukuljevich, keeper of the Croatian archives.

† There was long debate between Slavic scholars as to the relative antiquity of the Glagolitic and Cyrillic alphabets, and it has been but lately decided that the former is the oldest. To recommend it to the Court of Rome, it was said to have been invented by St Jerome; and now, to recommend it to the Slavs of the Oriental communion, the fact is insisted on that its origin dates from a period before the split between the Eastern and Western Churches.

‡ Introduced into Croatia by Dr Ljudevit Gaj.

Sultan tribute they should continue to administer their own affairs. Of course this condition became a dead letter so soon as the Turks got footing in the country; and partly from its proximity to Stamboul, partly because it lay on the march of Turkish armies to the Danube, few portions of the empire have seen the Christian more oppressed, or his spirit more broken, than Bulgaria. One step to this end was the abolition of the native Patriarchate, and the subjection of the Slavonic Christians to Greek bishops sent from Constantinople. This arrangement has subsisted ninety years; but in it the Bulgarians have never acquiesced, and their first unanimous and unflagging, though passive, resistance to Ottoman authority, has been made in a refusal to admit foreign bishops, or permit foreign interference with their schools.

Another means resorted to for holding down the Bulgarian is the introduction of Mohammedan colonists, who replenish the declining Mussulman population,* and are kept well supplied with arms, of which the Christian is deprived. Tatars from the Crimea were being tried while we were in the country; and since then, a fiercer and more fanatical instrument has been found in the Circassian.†

Under circumstances so disadvantageous, it is surprising how far the Bulgarian has been preserved from the vices of a conquered population in the East. His village is withdrawn from view of the highroad, to elude, if possible, the intrusion of Turkish violence. Even in the towns, his house is of insignificant exterior, for fear of attracting Turkish cupidity; but within his humble dwelling all is order and cleanliness: his field and his flower-garden are carefully tended, and his modest, virtuous helpmate is as praiseworthy for her tidiness and thrift as he is himself for honesty and diligence.‡ The Bulgarian is of dark

* The decrease of the Mussulman population in the "Province of Bulgaria," so-called (north of the Balkan), is estimated at 100,000 in ten years by Lieutenant-Colonel Neale, H.M. Consul in Bulgaria.—'Social Science Review,' February 1864.

† The idea has been adopted of planting Circassian colonists along the frontier of Serbia, so as to bar off the Bulgarians. We have ourselves seen how the Christian peasants were obliged to build huts and provide food for the newly-arrived Tartars; but the Tartars were only idle, whereas the Circassians come thirsting to avenge their own suffering on all who bear the Christian name. It has been said that, inasmuch as the Turk can neither govern nor conciliate a subject people, his only alternative is to *ruin* it.

‡ "As for the Bulgarians, whether they remain yet awhile under Turkish rule, or free themselves from it in our own time, as they must ultimately do sooner or later, it is in them alone that one can see any really hopeful prospect on taking a broad general view of the probable future of these countries. This is afforded by their numerical preponderance, their utter primitiveness, which has learned nothing and has nothing to unlearn; their industry and thrift, their obstinacy and their sobriety of character."—*Lord Strangford.*

complexion, large and strong limbed, but with a *down-look*
and a slouch; the women are comely, with fine teeth and
hair. In manner the Bulgarian is reserved and shrinking,
and to those whom he does not trust he opposes a shield of
dogged stupidity; but persons who have instructed him, either
in his own country or abroad, bear witness that his understand-
ing is excellent, and that he is eager and apt to learn. A great
number of young Bulgarians are now studying, at their own
cost, in Paris, Prague, St Petersburg, and Constantinople. On
their return home many will become schoolmasters; and thus
it is hoped that education may make its way in spite of the
jealousy of the Turkish Government and Greek priesthood,
which does not suffer a college, or even a printing-press, to be
started in any Bulgarian town.

We now turn to the Serbo-Croats, who form the western
division of the South Slavonic race. Of this people, Constan-
tine Porphyrogenitus informs us that they entered their present
lands in the seventh century, being invited thither by the
Emperor Heraclius to people his Mœsian provinces desolated by
the Avars. A district north of the Carpathians in Gallicia, and
thence eastward into Russia, is regarded by the Serbo-Croats as
their ancient home, and is said at one time to have borne the
names which they transferred to their new settlements. Unlike
the first Slavonic settlers of Bulgaria, the Serbo-Croats crossed
the Danube as an organised community, commanded by princes;
and, though afterwards they nominally recognised the Byzantine Emperor, they were never ruled except by their own chiefs.
This is remarkable, because to a certain extent the original
communal and municipal organisation still survives among the
Serbs, while the name Župan* (ruler of a district), which was
that borne by their first governors, is still used in Croatia to
express a municipal office of high rank.

The tribes which settled nearest the Bulgarians gave the
name of *Serbia* to their land, of which the south-eastern boundary
extended from the river Timok to the Adriatic at Antivari. The
Croats settled to the north and west. Hence it came that, on
their adoption of Christianity, the Serbs fell under the ecclesiastical jurisdiction of Byzance, the Croats under that of Rome—
an accident fraught with dissension and disaster after the separ-
ation of the Western from the Eastern Church.

The Croats had a separate monarchy till the beginning of the
twelfth century, when they placed their crown on the head
of the King of Hungary. It is now worn by the Emperor of

* Pronounce Ž as j in the French word *jour*—Joupaan.

Austria; but in all his dealings with the triune kingdom of Dalmatia, Slavonia, and Croatia, he is bound to use the title, not of Kaiser, but of King. Alliance with powerful neighbours saved Croatia from subjection to the Turks, with whom, however, she was constantly at war, almost to the present day. A still more savage enemy was repulsed by her in that horde of Mongols, which during the thirteenth century overran the whole of Hungary; but was brought to a stand by the Croats, and totally defeated on the field of Graves (Slav. Grobnik) near Fiume (1241).

Meanwhile, in the Serb provinces the great family of Nemania succeeded in raising a powerful state. Eight kings and three czars represent the flourishing period of Serbian monarchy, and by intermarriages with France, Venice, and Constantinople, brought the influence of the most civilised countries in Europe to bear upon their people. Such churches, frescoes, and MSS. as have escaped destruction, bear witness to the progress made by the Serbs in the thirteenth, fourteenth, and fifteenth centuries; the Museum of Belgrade preserves coins of Serb rulers from 1195 to 1457; and the code of laws promulgated in one of their great national assemblies still exists, to prove that in their courts of justice the meanest peasant could call to account the noble, the priest—nay, the czar.*

As the Serbian czardom grew the Greek empire was dwindling away, and in 1355 the Czar Stephen Dushan deemed it possible to take Constantinople, and unite Greeks and Slavons in one realm. Had he succeeded, and infused the vigour of his young northern peoples into the frame of an ancient civilisation, this portion of the old Roman Empire might, like the West, have witnessed a revival of national energy and classic culture, and the south-eastern peninsula might have become a second Italy. To defeat this scheme the Greek Emperor called in the hosts of the Ottoman, and we have the result in Turkey-in-Europe. A few days' journey to the north-west of Macedonian Edessa, lies a beautiful plain encircled by hills. This is the ill-fated field of Kossovo, where, in 1389, the Serbs staked and lost their empire, their army, and their czar. The very name of this battle is scarcely known in England, yet few have been more important, or in their consequences more disastrous to civilisation.

* A new and accurate translation of the so-called "Code of Czar Dushan" is now being made by command of the Prince of Serbia. It will first be rendered into German, and then into English. Documents bearing on the history of Serbia are to be found among the archives of Venice, and a collection including many old charters has lately been published. 'Monumenta Serbica, Miklosich.' Braumuller, Vienna. 1858.

The victory of the Moslem at Kossovo plunged the wide lands between the Black Sea and the Adriatic into the darkness of Turkish barbarism, and opened to the janissary the road to the Danube, Buda, and Vienna.

After the battle of Kossovo, the Serb rulers were called Princes and Despots, and paid tribute to the Sultan. The Turks were ostensibly their friends and allies ; but having once gained entrance to the country, they deprived the native rulers of one province after another, and finally drove them to cross the Danube. The last scion of the Serbian Princes was induced to call his people to arms in aid of an Austrian invasion of Turkey, and was then seized by order of the German Emperor, and kept a prisoner till his death, 1711.

But though the Serbian empire fell nearly 500 years ago, the Serbian people has never *said die*. Many of the inhabitants of the inland provinces, finding the contest in their own country hopeless, crossed the Danube, fought the Turk in the armies of the Emperor of Germany, and formed the celebrated military frontier. Again, a remnant of the Serbian nobility found a refuge on the mountain group of Zeta, which, under the name of Montenegro, continues a free Serbian state to this day. At length, in 1804, a million of Serbs dwelling near the Danube rose, and, after a struggle of thirty years, succeeded in winning for themselves their present autonomy, which has since been placed under European guarantee.

The Principality of Serbia pays an annual tribute to the Sultan, and is as yet obliged to tolerate a Turkish garrison in the Danubian fortresses. Otherwise her autonomy is complete, her government is administered by a native prince, assisted by ministers and a senate, besides the National Assembly (Skoupshtina), which must be called once in three years. The Skoupshtina is composed of deputies from districts and towns in the proportion of one deputy for every 2000 electors. The electors include every Serbian citizen above the age of thirty, and paying taxes.

The regular troops of Serbia do not exceed 4000, but she is defended by a militia of 200,000 free yeomen, well drilled and armed. Of this militia 50,496 are kept ready to march at a moment's notice.*

The populations of Bosnia, Herzegovina, and Stara Serbia, are the only Serbs still under Mohammedan administration. Their condition is an abyss of poverty and discontent. In Bosnia more

* 'La Serbie et le Pays Serbe;' 'Ubicini;' 'Revue des Deux Mondes,' May 1864; 'Serbia in 1863,' by Ph. Christich, Serbian Senator ; 'Macmillan's Magazine,' April 1863.

than two-thirds of the population are Christian, the greater number belonging to the Oriental, the smaller to the Roman Church ; these parties are now making up their quarrels on the common ground of nationality,* but hitherto their dissensions have left them fair game for the Mussulman. The Christians are peasants, artisans, or merchants ; the landholders are Slavonic Mussulmans, descendants of the old aristocracy who apostatised to save their estates and lives. These Mohammedans continue to speak Serbian, some few can read it, and even get at Slavonic journals ; while many are said to hold concealed their ancestors' patents of nobility, hoping to derive advantage from them whenever the tide shall turn. Till lately the so-called Beys ruled Bosnia in virtual independence ; and being then highly satisfied with their position, contributed the best janissaries to the Sultan's army, and held the country so stoutly against foreign invasion that they were called by Turkish writers the " Lion that guarded Stamboul." But no sooner did the Sultan's Government begin to admit European interference, and to abate somewhat of the Mohammedan's pride of place, than it lost all prestige among the Bosniac Mussulmans, who not only revolted, but called on the Christian population to join them in throwing off the foreign yoke. But the long - oppressed Christians would not trust them, and preferred listening to the promises of Omer Pasha, who put down the revolt, broke the power of the Beys, and placed the administration in the hands of Turkish officials. Since then the Mohammedan Bosniacs have become more hostile to the Turks than the Christians themselves ; the conscription cannot be raised among them, and as they habitually disdain labour, taxation reduces them to ruin and despair. As a counterpoise to the discontent of the native Mussulmans, it is necessary to conciliate the Christians ; hence to some extent the Porte really endeavours to ameliorate the condition of the Bosnian Rayah : but the situation is desperate, for the Christian's first use of strength will be to rid himself of

---

* This growing harmony between Christians of different denominations in Bosnia and Albania is favoured by the French Government, which causes its agents to set a good example to their Catholic co-religionists, by rendering cordial assistance to the Oriental Christians. The Empress Eugénie has contributed to the support of non-Catholic female schools, and Christians of the Orthodox Church begged us to repeat cases of oppression rather to the French than to the Russian Consul. On the other hand, Austria, the *soi-disant* protector of the Latin Christians in Bosnia and Albania, does all in her power to encourage sectarian rivalry, while she gives little assistance to any one, and is bitterly complained of even by her own *protégés*. Hence while the influence of France is gradually superseding that of Russia, a certain highly-placed personage frankly told the Cabinet of Vienna that Austrian agents did so much to favour the spread of Russian influence, that, at least in Bosnia, it was quite unnecessary for the Russian Government to pay agents of its own.

Mohammedan government; and in weakening and alienating the native Mussulmans, the Sultan has broken the only arm that could have repelled invasion or repressed revolt. It may be said here as elsewhere, that should the Porte indeed make good its promises of placing its Christian subjects on a level with the Mohammedan, it will thereby sever the bond of self-interest, by which Albanian or Slavonic Mussulmans have alone been attached to its rule. We saw more of the Bosnian Mussulmans than is usual among Frankish travellers, both because conciliating them by attempts to speak their own language, and as having access to their harems.

In the Herzegovina the Christians are more numerous in proportion, more vigorous and spirited, than those in Bosnia. They are considered the handsomest men among the Southern Slavs, and their dialect is the most beautiful in the language : as such, it has been selected for the modern translation of the New Testament, and for the published version of the national songs. The districts of the Herzegovina bordering on Montenegro are the scene of constant petty but bloody insurrections, which will only cease when the insurgents shall be subjected to some Government capable of keeping them in order, and interested in improving their condition. It has been remarked* that "Montenegro has a natural though limited line of probable annexation on her north-western frontier, in the border Christian districts of the Herzegovina, towards Niksich and Trebinge." In the interest of all parties it is to be wished that this natural annexation should be effected as soon as possible, for at present the frontier of Montenegro leaves outside it tribes whom it certainly ought to include if a Montenegrine frontier be recognised at all. These tribes are Christian, and will not suffer the presence of Mussulmans. In war they follow the standard of the Black Mountain, in peace their disputes are referred to the tribunal of Cetigne; yet if oppressed rayahs in the low country call on them for help, if on their own account they make a raid on the adjacent champaigns, or if it suits their mountain neighbours to incite them to disturbance,—in short, do what they may,—the Prince of Montenegro cannot be called to account, for they are no subjects of his. Meanwhile the Turkish authorities in Herzegovina do not even pretend to control the clans on the frontier, nor to protect peaceful people from their depredations ; so that, were those clans regularly included in Montenegro, the Sultan would not hereby lose a single subject, nor would the fighting force of the Prince be swelled by the accession of one man whose service he does not

* Lord Strangford.

already command. On the other hand, by making the Prince responsible for the behaviour of these borderers, several districts of the Herzegovina would cease to be a battle-ground between Turkish troops and rayah guerillas, who now plunder them in turn. Montenegro has again and again demanded a rectification of her frontier, and again and again satisfaction has been promised. If what must be done ultimately were done at once, Turkey would be rid of a source of disputes which are certain to be raked up the first time she happens to have too much on her hands to keep up a large army on the Montenegrīne borders.*

As for Montenegro itself, the valour by which its self-government has been preserved is scarcely more remarkable than its history and origin. At an early date the south of the Herzegovina, and the north-west of Albania as far as Durazzo, were included in the Serbian government of Zeta, of which the capital was Dioclea, an old Roman settlement on the lake of Scutari. Zeta was the original appanage of the Nemania family; and after they had extended their rule to the Danube it became the fief of the second person of the empire, usually of the heir-apparent to the throne. The famous Stephen Dushan is said to have held this government during the life of his father, and the northern Albanians to have been as much attached to him as his Serbs.†

* It will, however, be necessary to instruct the Commissioners intrusted with this rectification, that the thing expected of them is to obviate future grounds of dispute, and not, as heretofore, merely to display in puppet-show the jealousies of certain European cabinets. Last time the frontier was defined, those of the Commissioners who made it a point of honour to stickle for every inch of soil on behalf of Turkey, achieved drawing the boundary in some districts so as to divide the lands of a tribe or of a village. Thus they left behind them quarrels ready made, on account of which the Porte has had to defend worthless bits of ground at a considerable expenditure of money and troops.

† It is remarkable that dissensions between Serbs and Albanians are not traceable in the history of these regions, until it became the interest of Mussulman conquerors to set one Christian race against another. The written laws of Serbian Czars speak of Serbs and Albanians, whether Orthodox or Catholic, as subjects of one realm ; and when the southern parts of the Serbian empire broke up into independent states, we find Albanian chiefs in alliance with Serbian against the Turks. At present the numbers of the Albanians, all in all, must be nearer one than two millions ; and, as every one knows, the Northern Albanians, or Gheggas, are divided by many characteristics, and by the strongest animosity, from the Southern Albanians or Toskes. The Southern Albanians colonise a great part of modern Greece, and easily become Graecised : in their own country many of them speak Greek as well as their mother tongue. The Northern Albanians, on the contrary, are to a great extent interspersed with Serbian and Bulgarian populations, and in addition to their own tongue speak Slavic. Except those in the Turkish service, even the Mohammedans among them do not speak Turkish, and, like the Slavonic Mohammedans in Bosnia, they hate the very sound of it. Nothing can be looser than the tenure by which

36

When the strength of the czardom was broken, several of its provinces assumed independence, and among others Zeta under the family of Balsha, and afterwards under that of Cernoïevich —both connected with the ruling house of Serbia.* Ivan Cernoïevich defended his patrimony against the Turks until 1489, when, finding the low country untenable, he abandoned his castle Zabliak, on the north shore of the lake of Scutari, and took up his position in the alpine plain of Cetigne. His warriors followed him, swearing on the New Testament to remain true to their nation and their faith, and to chase from among them, girded with a woman's apron, whoever should dare to counsel surrender. The standard on the Black Mountain of Zeta—or, as the Venetians called it, Montenegro—became the rallying-point for all unconquered spirits in Serbia, and especially for such of the old nobility as neither apostatised nor were massacred.

These immigrants, highbred and, for the times, civilised, transmitted to their descendants the characteristics which have distinguished them above their equally warlike neighbours, the Roman Catholic Albanians. 1st, Though the greater part of the Mountain has twice been temporarily overrun by Mussulmans, its chief has never stooped to even a nominal recognition of the Sultan as suzerain. 2d, Among its traditions has been preserved the definite expectation of returning to the position of a civilised nation. 3d, Its rugged warriors have a genuine respect for culture, and demand it in their leaders. Their ruler has almost always been a person of some European education, and, in one instance, of high literary attainment.† One of the earliest typographies in these countries was set up in Montenegro ; and when that site became untenable, a Montenegrine—or, as he is styled, a noble of Zeta—established a printing-press for Serbian books at Venice, for which service to civilisation he was created Baron of the Holy Roman Empire by the Emperor Charles V.

The Cernoïevich were no more, and the government of Montenegro had passed to its metropolitan or Vladika, when the powerful family of Nïegush immigrated from the Herzegovina,

the Albanians hold the Moslem creed, or indeed any creed ; their professions of religion are dictated wholly by interest, and to this day certain districts change to and fro according as they are most anxious to avoid paying *haratch* as Christians, or giving men to the conscription as Turks.

* See 'Dalmatia and Montenegro,' by Sir Gardner Wilkinson. See also 'Slavische Alterthumer.'—Shafarick. 'Souveranité du Montenegro.'—Vaclik. The Histories of Serbia in Serbian and German.

† The last Vladika, Peter II. of Nïegush, a man of European education, and the author of many remarkable poems, some of which were published in Vienna, some in his own monastery. He acutely felt his isolation among an uncivilised community, and used to describe himself as the hermit of Cetigne.

and rose to the leadership of the struggling state. Daniel of Nïegush became Vladika of Montenegro, and saved it from the greatest danger it ever ran from the Turks. In reward his office was made hereditary in the family, and has remained with it to the present day. In 1850 his descendant Danilo separated the secular from the ecclesiastical dignity, and resumed the title of Prince.

Chief of the only body of Serbians who never recognised a foreign master, scion of a strong-willed and gifted family that has ruled for nearly two hundred years, the present young Prince of Montenegro holds a position which, in the estimation of the greater part of the Southern Slavs, must distance every other candidate to future headship of the race, although the greater age and experience of the present ruler of Danubian Serbia secures the first place to him so long as he lives.* Last winter various Slavonic organs were clamorous for the public adoption of Prince Nicholas as heir of the Prince of Serbia, but as yet the only earnest of possible promotion has reached him in the form of attempts at assassination, the perpetrators being known enemies of his family, who find shelter and pensions in the territory of his neighbours.

The present monastery of Cetigne preserves in its wall a tablet taken from the ruins of the original foundation, and sculptured with the two-headed eagle of Serbia. The present chief of

---

* The family of Nïegush have ever been careful to make known that no personal claims of theirs shall form a ground of rivalry or dispute. During the late war with Turkey, Prince Nicholas of Montenegro constantly declared before his warriors that if only Prince Michael of Serbia would take the field, he was ready to serve as his first soldier. Lately he has requested the Prince of Serbia to stand sponsor to his first-born child. There are many Montenegrines settled in Serbia, and many emigrate thither every year. Unlike those who go for work to Constantinople, who always eventually return home, those who go to Serbia remain there and adopt it as their country, although it takes a course of years to accustom them to peaceful pursuits.

Ubicini says—"La condition essentielle du succès, c'est que ces petites unités s'absorberont dans les grandes, que le Montenegro sera annexé à la Serbie et non la Serbie au Montenegro. Par le Montenegro, accru des bouches du Cattaro, territoire entièrement serbe, la Serbie touchera dès lors à l'Adriatique, et communiquant librement avec l'Europe, sera sûre de son developpement commercial et politique, car la mer, les ports, sont l'appareil respiratoire des nations : privées de ce débouché necessaire, elles peuvent bien defendre leur liberté à l'abri des rochers et des montagnes, elles ne peuvent ni s'etendre ni prosperer ; elles ne font que durer en demeurant stationnaires.

"Comment donc se réalisera l'union Serbo-Monténégrine? C'est une question qu'il ne faut qu'indiquer, et il serait téméraire d'essayer d'y repondre. Le Prince Michel n'a malheureusement pas d'enfans ; on parle d'une adoption qui placerait après lui sur le trône de Serbie un prince de la famille de Nïegush. Ce qui est certain, c'est que l'adoption est bien dans les mœurs slaves, témoins les Obrénonovich eux-mêmes : cet Obren, dont la dynastie régnante a emprunté le nom, c'etait le beau-père et non le père de Milosh."—' Revue des deux Mondes,' 15 Mai 1864.

the Black Mountain has adopted the family arms of Ivan Cernoïevich. The significance of Montenegro in the eyes of the
Southern Slavs is as the link that connects their old world with
their present hopes and aims.

.   .   .   .

It so happened that our journey through the Principality of
Serbia took place immediately after the bombardment of Belgrade, at the moment when the national militia was called out.
In Montenegro we have been several times before and after the
late war. We had therefore many opportunities of seeing large
bodies of men in good array, and can fully endorse the opinion
of late travellers, that the Serbian population is physically mag-
nificent—tall and stalwart in frame, broad-browed, and of noble
bearing.*

In the Principality the common dress consists of a white
linen tunic and leggings, a sleeveless vest, a scarlet cap, and a
scarlet woollen girdle worn over a leather one, in which are carried a pair of pistols and a hangiar. Richer yeomen and merchants wear jacket, waistcoat, and knickerbockers of cloth, the
jacket lined with fur and often embroidered. The costume of
the peasant women has endless variety; but those in the towns
are adopting the French dress, and a gold-embroidered jacket, a
long sash, and round headdress, are all that remain of the
national style.

In the Turkish provinces the Serb Christians must not wear
arms, nor exhibit garments of too bright a hue. The women,
indeed, behind the protection of closed doors, do in the towns dare
to dress themselves in long robes trimmed with sable and gold,
and neck-loads of ducats and pearls. The Bosnian Mohammedan
retains the Eastern dress which young Turkey has exchanged for
a monkey-like imitation of Europe. But many of the old Beys
are now growing so poor that they give to the melting-pot such
jewels and rich arms as escaped the plunder of Omer Pasha, and
the introduction of modern weapons is taking their last value
from silver-mounted pistols and guns inlaid with mother-of-pearl.

The oldest and most characteristic bit of South Slavonic
costume is to be found among the Montenegrines, in a long,

* Dr Sandwith.
"L'expression de tristesse qui assombrit la physionomie du paysan roumain,
cette apathie qu'on lui reproche, font place, chez le Serbe, a un air de franchise
et de dignité naturelle qui frappe tous les voyageurs."—Ubicini.
"La confiance dit quelque part M. Guillaume Lejean, que le dernier de ces
paysans a en lui-même et en sa race se trahit dans son allure, dans sa démarche
preste et allègre, dans son langage à la fois coloré, harmonieux et viril." Le
révérend W. Denton résume son éloge par cette phrase : "Chaque Serbe est un
gentleman."— 'Revue des deux Mondes,' 15 Mai 1864.

gold-embroidered coat of peculiar form, which is said to have descended from the Court of the Stephens.* And the cap of the Montenegrines has a story of its own. Its crown is crimson, with one corner worked in gold. The broad red field represents fatal Kossovo; the golden corner is the free Montenegro. Around the brim they wear a black band, in mourning for such Serbian tribes as yet endure the Turkish yoke.

As to disposition, the Serbo-Croat shares with the Bulgarian his sentiments of nationality and tenacity of purpose; but, unlike the Bulgarian, he is warlike, and whether Christian or Mohammedan, Austrian borderer or janissary, Bosnian Bey or Montenegrine, he has secured respect for his stubborn valour. The Christian tribes are still more honourably distinguished by their deference to the defenceless,—a woman is to them inviolable, and the stranger under her protection safe. The gifts of eloquence and improvisatory poetry are generally diffused among the Serbs. Their struggle for national existence is recorded in a series of ballads sung from hearth to hearth down through five centuries to the present day.† Hanging to the door of the wayside inn, we often found a small guitar (Slav. gusla), and in absence of the professional blind singer, it was handed to the eldest man present, or to him most distinguished for warlike deeds.

But those qualities which render the Serbo-Croat more interesting than the Bulgarian, are balanced by serious practical defects. He is averse to labour, impatient, careless, and, though quick at learning, is troublesome to teach. Especially he differs from the Bulgarian in this, that *nothing can be got out of him by oppression.* The Croatian peasant was, the Dalmatian Morlack and the Bosnian rayah still are, the laziest, sulkiest, most intractable, most implacable of mortals. Such merchants as succeed in Bosnia come *not* of the crushed Christians in that province, but from the insurgent districts in Herzegovina. In free Montenegro theft is all but unknown, and in Serbia every man wears arms without danger to the public peace; but in Dalmatia, not all that Austrian police and soldiers can do will keep down brigandage or root out the Vendetta.

We have alluded to the fact that traces of old communal organisation yet survive among the Serbs. It will be a sad mistake if, in haste to be civilised, they should blot these out, and squeeze their sturdy little Principality into the strait-waistcoat of a bureaucracy. No doubt, however, some of the good

---

* The name Stephan—*i.e.*, the Crowned—was adopted on their accession by all or nearly all the Kings and Czars of Serbia.

† See four volumes of Serbian national songs, edited by Vuk Karadshich.

old ways are somewhat embarrassing to a modern Administration. For instance, up to the present hour the Serbian yeoman has successfully resisted the intrusion of the tax-gatherer; his poll-tax, nominally one pound per householder, being collected and apportioned by the elders of each Commune. Lately the Prince of Serbia declared the revenue thus raised to be unequal to the expenses of the State, and proposed the substitution of a regular tax on property. In the National Assembly held the other day, he announces that this measure has as yet proved impracticable. It is not to pay more that the people refuse, but they choose to raise it in their own way.

II. Our first journey through the South Slavonic countries led us down the eastern shore of the Adriatic, and then up to that unique capital, the Montenegrine Cetigne. The neighbouring Turkish port, Antivari, was shown us as the farthest point to the southward inhabited on this coast by the Slavonic race. Montenegro herself has no port, and scarcely a plain of arable land — advantages unwisely withheld from her by Turkey and Austria, since if the mountaineer could gain a peaceful livelihood he would naturally lose his taste for war. The abundance of fine harbours on the Slavic shore of the Adriatic contrasts with the lack of them on the opposite coast of Italy, and makes it the more deplorable that the countries inland should be separated from these their natural ports. The people frequently remark with bitterness, that Dalmatia without Bosnia and the Herzegovina is a face without a head.* For the Montenegrines, the true harbour is the Bocche di Cattaro, whose shores are inhabited by people of their own race, and whose waters wash the foot of their hills. In 1814 the place was actually made over to them by the English in return for their assistance in dislodging the French. But Russia forced them to resign it to her, and then transferred it to Austria. They now ask, at least, the little bay of Spizza, which nominally belongs to Turkey, but is overlooked by their territory, and made no use of by the Turks or any one else. By way of satisfying them, they have been allowed to import free at Antivari

* See 'Highlands and Islands of the Adriatic,' by A. A. Paton, now Consul at Ragusa. At the time of our journey this gentleman was the only British Consul in these parts acquainted with any South Slavonic tongue. The Prussian Consul at Ragusa spoke Serbian, and from that circumstance, as well as from a liberality of view towards the Slavonic race somewhat unusual among Germans, he was greatly beloved in that part of the world. We have to thank him for much courtesy and useful information; but not long after our departure, the death of his accomplished wife (a Ragusan lady of high family) so afflicted him as to occasion his withdrawal from general society, a loss already felt by visitors to Ragusa.

all articles not used in the manufacture of arms or gunpowder;
but the exception serves as an excuse for prying into any cargo;
and we found the green tents of Turkish soldiers pitched down
to the water's edge. The port of Antivari is also separated by
high ranges from Cetigne; and to reach it from the nearest
point of Montenegro it is necessary to traverse Turkish ground.
Our second journey was from Constantinople across central
Bulgaria to Belgrade.

The third route started from Belgrade, traversed the Principality of Serbia, and two Turkish provinces inhabited by Serbs,
i.e., Bosnia and Herzegovina. We crossed the frontier between
Turkey and Austria, and reached the coast of the Adriatic at
Ragusa.

The fourth journey started from Thessalonica, and proceeded
inland to Monastir—Slav. *Bitolia;* thence northward to the
frontier of the Principality, where we turned to the south-west
and traversed a district called by the Turks *Arnaoutluk,* and
by its Christian inhabitants Stara—*i.e.*, Old Serbia. Having
reached the chief town of this region, Prizren, formerly the
Serbian capital, we passed through the hills of northern Albania, and arrived at Scutari, Skodra, or Skadar, on the lake of
that name.

Our fifth route departed from Trieste —a point where the
South Slavonic population meets the Italian. We passed
through the *Slovene* country and its chief town, Laybach (Slav.
Liubliana), into the kingdom of Croatia, and from thence through
Slavonia till we again found ourselves in Belgrade, at the junc-
tion of the rivers Danube and Save.

We also made an excursion to Sirmium, or, as it is called, the
Frusca Gora, a hilly peninsula between the Danube and Save,
interesting from its monasteries, most of which were built by
Christian emigrants from Turkey. Among other relics they
transported thither the body of their last Czar, who in his youth
was Count of Sirmium, and ever retained his title of Knes
Lazar. For the last two centuries there has been no stronger
hold of Serbian patriotism than the Frusca Gora, although its
capital, Carlovitz, the residence of the Patriarch, is seldom given
into the keeping of any one but a creature of the Austrian
Government. The Serbians settled in the Banat of Hungary
are also most tenacious of their national characteristics; they
claim to live under a voivode of their own, and to use their own
language in all government transactions. As this self-assertion
is not taken in good part either by Austria or Hungary, many
of their young men prefer to serve under the National Government of the Principality of Serbia; and it is frequently declared

that, should the districts from which their ancestors emigrated ever be restored to Christian rule, numbers will leave the north bank of the Danube and return to their fatherland.

We may mention that in the Slavonic countries of Austria, and generally in the Principality of Serbia, we performed our journeys in a carriage or in a light four-wheeled cart; through the plains of Bulgaria in a covered waggon without seats or springs ; everywhere else on horseback. In the districts ruled by Turkish officials the roads were bad beyond the worst one sees in other parts of Europe ; the most tolerable being that from Brod on the Save to Saraïevo, capital of Bosnia, and a bit between Sophia and Nish, which was made to transport cannon during the alarm of an outbreak in Serbia. Even where highways and bridges have once been, they are allowed to become useless for want of repair. Strange to say, throughout Turkey in Europe communication by telegraph has preceded that by road. But even this is not in the best of order. When crossing the mountains between Bosnia and Herzegovina our horses were nearly tripped up by what seemed to be a cord trailing in the forest. It proved to be the telegraph wire, of which the nearest supports had been blown down.

Throughout all the Turkish provinces we were obliged to travel with guards, their numbers varying from three or four to twenty and upwards. When you cross into Serbia this precaution becomes unnecessary.

Within the Principality of Serbia we found society in a primitive stage ; and the cultivator, having few wants, is more contented than industrious. But life and property are secure ; all members of the community are equal before law; the dues of the clergy are fixed, and the judges above suspicion of bribery.* When brigandage shows itself, as it does from time to time in mountainous districts, and especially on the Turkish border, it

* To guard against official corruption Serbia pays her officials well, and, by the account of those who have known the life of the lower class of Government employés both in Austria and Serbia, and judge with regard to the relative price and style of living, the little principality provides for her servants better than the great empire. The means adopted by the Serbs to put an end to the demoralisation both of officials and ecclesiastics, which prevailed in their country while it was under the Turks, are worthy of the attention of most of the nations in east Europe.
Increased intercourse with foreign nations, the introduction of foreign luxuries and artificial wants, transition from the life of primitive yeomen to that of citizens of Belgrade, all are contributing to raise the value of riches in Serbia. Industry will thus be increased, but integrity and simplicity of character will become more difficult. The calling-out of the militia is regarded by many Serbians as a great benefit to the country, reviving the old hardy spirit, and supplying townsfolk and country-folk with a common ground of meeting.

is summarily suppressed, and the country population assists the Government to hunt down the thieves. In a district which had been recently disturbed we saw an axe lying where it had been purposely left in the forest, and where it had lain for weeks without any one daring to meddle with it.

On the Mohammedan side of the frontier we found the judges and all officials venal, and the extortions of the Christian clergy backed by the still more extortionate Turkish governors. At the time of our journey neither life nor property was secure— not even for Franks, nor on the most frequented thoroughfares. The servant of a British Consul, having offended the Mussulmans of a town, was killed by their firing a volley into his master's lodging; and a month afterwards, when we saw the Consul, he was still unable to bring punishment on the murderers. An American missionary with whom we were acquainted was plundered and murdered by brigands in open day, and on the post-road between Constantinople and Belgrade; a fortnight later we were almost prevented from traversing the same highway by the difficulty of finding trustworthy guards. The chief points wherein injustice is suffered by the native Christians appeared to be the following: As a rule, their evidence is not received in courts of justice; they are disarmed, whereas the Mussulmans are armed; obstacles are placed in the way of their holding land or buying land that has ever belonged to a Mussulman; by one means or another they are made to pay far more than their share of the taxes; their women are liable to be violently carried off, and a Turk who can gain possession of a Christian girl and induce her to become a Mohammedan, so far from being punished, is in some districts rewarded by exemption from the conscription. Christians are also exposed to be murdered by Mussulmans, without the murderers being brought to justice. In and around Ochrida, Monastir, and Perlepe;* at Ipek, in Old Serbia, and at Mostar, in the Herzegovina, we had certain information on this head. An American missionary told us that near Eski Sagra, in Bulgaria, where he was stationed, from seventy to one hundred Christians were killed annually by Mussulmans without inquiry being made. Reference to residents in the country will suffice to confirm these statements; such instances as came under our own notice occurred between January 1862-1864; the British Ambassador at Constantinople was Sir Henry Bulwer, and the Grand Vizier was Fuad Pasha.

In the course of our journeys we satisfied ourselves of a fact which has more than once been questioned, and remained un-

* Recently confirmed by the statements made by Mrs Walker in her inter-esting work, 'Through Macedonia to the Albanian Lakes.'

answered for want of information. From the Black Sea to the Adriatic, from the mouth of the Vardar to the Danube, the mass of the population speaks, as its native language, the *Slavonic* tongue. To this rule Mohammedans in Bosnia, and many of those in Bulgaria, form no exception. Four hundred years ago they gave up their fathers' creed; they would never give up their fathers' speech. Further, we convinced ourselves that the Slavonic tongue spoken in these regions has only two dialects of which the divergence is at all considerable. These two are the Serbo-Croat and the Bulgarian;* but even in them the difference lies in grammatical construction, their vocabulary being the same. Of their practical resemblance we made some trials:—1st, Having learned to read the national songs of Serbia, which are in the language of the common people, we tried to read a popular song of Bulgaria, and found that we could make out almost every word. 2dly, It happened to us twice to pass from Bulgarian into Serb districts with servants who knew no Slavonic tongue except Bulgarian : on both occasions we found they conversed freely with the Serbs, alike in the Principality and Montenegro.

We must also give our testimony that the Southern Slavs are everywhere desirous to rise in the scale of civilisation, and striving to give their children an education that will fit them for a higher stage of political life. In Croatia and Serbia much has lately been done for public instruction ; but even in those Turkish provinces where the Christians occupy the lowest social position, and receive neither assistance nor encouragement from the Mohammedan Government, they have started schools in all their larger towns, and sent young men intended for schoolmasters to be trained in Paris, Prague, and Russia. And all this is done in a *national*-spirit ; for, split up as they are under divers political systems, these peoples are certainly cultivating a sense of their national oneness, and are desirous to represent it by a national literature, a national church, and ultimately by political union under a native ruler. This desire is inflamed by the consciousness that Austria, no less than Turkey, regards the development of her Slavonic provinces with jealousy, and has ever treated them with injustice. It is not unnatural that the inhabitants of a fine country, washed by two seas, should believe that they could attain prosperity if rid of hostile or stupid

* The dialect of the *Slovenes* who occupy the space intervening between Croatia and Italy has at present a literature distinct from the Serbo-Croat, but so small that efforts are now on foot to make one literary language serve both peoples. In some respects the Slovene dialect shows more resemblance than either Serbian or modern Bulgarian to the old Slavonic, which is the ecclesiastical language of the whole race.

masters, and free to develop their own powers in their own
way. The geographical position of these lands, with Venice,
Hungary, and Greece for their next neighbours, exposes them
to be kindled to insurrection by sparks which fly over their
frontiers as from a burning house to the nearest hay-rick, while
the fellow-feeling entertained for them by Russia, France, and
free Italy, shows that, should the Southern Slavs ever be able to
make head against their adversaries, they will not want for sympathy, nor even for allies.

At present, one of the means most looked to for giving an
impulse to civilisation is the increase of commercial relations
with Great Britain. On this account we propose to enter into
some particulars as to the products, capabilities, and geography
of these lands.

III. The South Slavonic countries are for the most part mountainous, but abound in fertile plains, among which may be instanced those of northern Bulgaria and of Thrace, of Sophia,
Samakov, and Salonica; and in "Old Serbia," the renowned fields
of Kossovo and Metochia. At one corner of Kossovo stands the
high pyramidal mountain Luibatrn, and immediately behind
Metochia, the hills of Herzegovina and northern Albania cul-
minate in that rocky knot called the Black Mountain or Montenegro. Its highest peaks, Kom and Dormitor, rise to between
eight and nine thousand feet. Thence branch to the westward
the long lines of Dinaric, Carnic, and Julian Alps.

In Bulgaria the principal chains are the Despoto-Dagh (Rho-
dope) and the Balkan (Hæmus), which formed the boundary of
ancient Thrace.

The Kopaunik, a hill of no great height on the southern
frontier of Serbia, is famous for the view it commands over the
lands between Macedonia and the Danube; but no prospect so
impressed us as that from Lovchen, the mountain-peak above
Cetigne, selected as the site of a church and the tomb of the
last Vladika.* From this point Montenegro appears like a petri-

* Peter II., previously alluded to. Lady Strangford, in her amusing account of
a visit to Montenegro, says that this church on Lovchen contains the tomb of
Peter I., whom the Montenegrines have declared a saint; and adds, "some
years after his death, his body was removed from Tsetinje to the summit of
the highest mountain in Montenegro, under the poetical idea that his people,
who can see this peak from every part of the country, would thus evermore remain under the protecting guardianship of their beloved chief." Unfortunately
this pretty and romantic description is founded on a misapprehension. The
Vladika interred on the mountain is the poet Peter II.; and St Peter's body
lies exposed to view in the chapel of the monastery of Cetigne, receiving the
homage of numerous pilgrims, whom it attracts even from beyond the frontier.
It was there seen by Sir G. Wilkinson, Mr Paton, and many other travellers

fied ocean, its waves rising literally "mountains high." Here and there among the billows you espy islets, tiny plains,—nay, often mere patches of cultivation dotted with the dwellings of the inhabitants. It is said that when the soil is washed away from the smallest and highest of these rock-gardens, it is replaced by the Montenegrine women, who climb to the ledges carrying burdens of earth on their backs. After once viewing Montenegro from the peak of Lovchen, one feels that the defence which the heroic mountaineers have maintained for centuries against the Mussulman is less desperate than their struggle with inhospitable nature.

The mountains of Bulgaria yield iron in abundance, and at some places, such as Samakov, it is worked, but in the most barbarous style. We have seen iron from England being transported on horseback to towns in the neighbourhood of these mines.

In the days of the Serbian empire it is known that considerable riches were derived from silver mines. Those most celebrated were Novo Berdo and Rudnik; and in the Rudnik hills may still be found the traces of a city and of the Roman Catholic chapel used by miners who came from Germany.* It is said that even within the narrow bounds of the present Principality are contained gold, silver, and copper, besides iron, lead, coal, saltpetre, sulphur,—everything necessary to the manufacture of arms and of gunpowder.

The South Slavonic countries are watered on the north by the large rivers Danube, Drave, and Save, with their tributaries;† on the south-east by the Maritza, the Vardar, and the Strymon, which fall into the Ægean. But on the south-west need is felt of a navigable outlet to the Adriatic; and last autumn the Austrian Consul Hahn made an expedition in hopes of ascertaining that the river Drina could be used for small steamers, and thus open up the fine woods of Stara-Serbia and Northern Albania. It is said that, after careful investigation, he was obliged to relinquish the idea. We had previously been riding for some days along the banks of the Drina, and could not but prognosticate the disappointment of the Consul from what we

besides ourselves. St Peter of Montenegro is one of the most modern saints of the Serb people. In old times many of their sovereigns were canonised, and the bodies of some of them are still shown laid out in open coffins. Lazar, the last Czar, lies in the monastery of Ravanitza, in Sirmium, and is supposed to wear a part of the dress in which he fell at Kossovo.
* Coins of these cities, and of Prizren and Skopia, may be seen in the Museum of Belgrade.
† Supplying the people with abundance of fish—in the mountain-rivers various species of the salmo, and in the plains with the siluris, lensis perca, sterlet, carp, eels, &c.--H. S.

saw of the shallowness of the water, and the prominence of rocks in the bed of the stream.

In *vegetable products*, the South Slavonian countries vary according to their variety of climate and soil. On the sunlit but rocky coast of the Adriatic we found the olive, the vine, the fig, but little else; in central Bulgaria there are vast rice-fields; in northern Bulgaria, cereals. All the warmer regions produce mulberry-trees, which serve for the rearing of silkworms; and during the late disease, a Greek merchant told us that silk seed from the valleys of Montenegro, when tested with other kinds at Milan, had proved the healthiest and best.

As for *wood*, the Balkan and the mountains of Serbia, Bosnia, and Croatia, are covered with forests of oak, beech, and fir. On the acorns of Serbian oakwoods are fattened vast herds of swine, an article of export found to be so profitable during the late Crimean war, that the country was almost drained of them, and has not yet recovered. On our rides through the forests we used to see these pigs careering about more like wild animals than fatted porkers. Even when pronounced ready for market, they have to travel to the Danube on foot, and thence by steamer and sometimes by rail to the town where they are killed. It is calculated that their value would be greatly increased if they could be converted into pork nearer home. No Serbian has yet ventured on this speculation, so it still stands open to foreign enterprise.

The new *cotton-field* alluded to we met with in South-eastern Bulgaria, especially about the town of Seres, and between it and Salonica. At the instigation of Great Britain, the Turkish Government has lately been induced to encourage the growth of cotton, giving seed to be sown, and, what is more important, suspending in favour of cotton some of the harassing taxation and interference which ruin industry in that part of the world. The Christian Bulgarians have responded to this encouragement in a manner that gives fair promise of their energies, should they ever be entirely delivered from the vexatious yoke of the Turk. The British Consul of Thessalonica told us that, between the years 1861 and 1862, exports of cotton had nearly doubled, and in the present year increased more than threefold. One man near Seres sowed three-quarters of an acre with cotton, and made a profit of £60. Great part of the plain of Salonica lies at present almost useless, but it is said to be particularly favourable for sea-island cotton. Many were the wishes that an English company would undertake its cultivation.

But the enterprise which awaits British capital in the South Slavonic countries is to make the railway between Salonica and

Belgrade, by which, as we have already said, our postal distance from India would be considerably shortened. The distance between Alexandria and Trieste is 1200 geographical miles; between Alexandria and Salonica only 670 miles; and, as compared with the Marseilles route, it has been calculated that, *via* Salonica, the Indian mail would take the same time to get from Alexandria to London that it now takes (by at least every second steamer) to get from Alexandria to Marseilles. The projected railway would be carried along the plains and valleys of the Morava and Vardar (Axius); the route, as it has been traced, crosses no important elevations, and its only engineering obstacles consist in some narrow river-defiles. The proportion of difficult parts to easy has been estimated as 1 to 9½, and the cost of the line (in Austrian money) as nearer 20,000,000 than 30,000,000 of florins—*i.e.*, nearer £2,000,000 than £3,000,000 sterling.

Regarding the present state of communications, an Austrian steamer connects Salonica with Syra; but between Salonica and the Danube, until you cross the Serbian frontier, there is not (or was not when we traversed it about a year ago) a single road over which it is bearable to pass in a wheeled vehicle. The journey is made by a riding post in 138 hours.

As for the great river-port, Belgrade—in commerce as in war the key of the East, and pointed out by an eminent British free-trader* as one of the future free ports of Europe—at present the malice of Turkey and of Austria combine to render it all but useless. The guns of a Turkish fortress command its streets; the late treacherous bombardment has destroyed all security, all possibility of merchants investing capital within the town; while the Austrians, on whose steamer the traveller is dependent for reaching the nearest railway station at Basiash, contrive, by inconvenient regulations as to time, fare, and customs, to render passage to and from Belgrade as vexatious and expensive as possible. There is, however, a Belgian Company which proposes to make a railway connecting *Fiume* (a port on the upper Adriatic) with *Semlin* on the Danube, opposite Belgrade. Should this line be carried on from Semlin to Basiash, and have a station on the Serbian shore, and a steamer to cross the river Save, Belgrade would be placed in direct relation by rail at once with the North Sea and the Adriatic, and travellers might escape those attentions which now await them from the Austrian police at Semlin.

Some years ago, when the Austrian Government had a creature of its own as Prince of Serbia, and thought to use him as a tool for extending its influence over the Slavonic population of

* Mr Cobden.

Turkey, it seriously entertained the idea of making a railroad between Belgrade and Thessalonica; and the learned and indefatig-
able Austrian Consul, M. Hahn, was commissioned to examine the
line of country. At Belgrade he acquired a travelling companion
in the person of an artillery officer in the Serbian service, who was
able to speak in their own language with the populations through
which the journey lay. After accompanying the Consul to Salonica, this officer returned to Belgrade alone, confirming and elu-
cidating his views by a second journey over the same ground.
M. Hahn published a valuable work on the subject. The Serbian officer kept his own notes, and is willing to place them
at the disposal of a Company that would entertain the idea
of carrying out the line. For it is by no means desired by the
Serbs and Bulgarians that a railroad traversing their country
should be in the keeping of Austria. They already know what
it is to have their letters to France and England opened and
detained because they must needs pass through an Austrian
post-office. They have heard of travellers being arrested by
Austrian police at the Cracow terminus. They foresee, too, that
whenever Austria might feel disposed to meddle in the internal
troubles of Turkey, the railroad would be used, not for commercial purposes, but for the transport of certain white-uniformed
troops. These are sufficient reasons why the South Slavonic
peoples should be anxious to have the line between Belgrade
and Salonica safe in the hands of a genuine Trading Company,
rather than in those of a Germanising government. Besides, a
great benefit might be conferred on the labouring population, if
the work were to be conducted on English principles. The
Bulgarians, through whose land it would chiefly pass, are a
thrifty, hard-working people, and nothing would tend to develop
their useful qualities like regular employment and regular pay.
At present, neither the one nor the other is to be had, nor do
they anywhere see the edifying and encouraging spectacle of a
work honestly and thoroughly carried out. As an instance of
the way things are done in Turkey: Some time ago the Pasha of
Salonica announced that he was about to make a road between
that city and Monastir, and to this end must raise a certain sum,
out of which all expenses should be defrayed. The work was
opened with pomp, and called the Imperial Highway; the contribution was paid in; but instead of being expended on the
road, it was put into the Pasha's pocket; the road was made
by forced labour, and in such a style, that during the heat of
summer we preferred riding to being jolted over its ruts. In
winter, it is all but impassable from mud.*

* This little anecdote applies more or less to every part of the Turkish Em-

D

IV. We will conclude these Notes on the South Slavonic countries with a word or two about such of their *cities* as are most worth consideration.

Perhaps the most interesting is *Ragusa (Dubrovnik)*, on the eastern or Slavic shore of the Adriatic, which, till taken by Napoleon, and since handed over to Austria, was a republic, answering in miniature to Venice. On the island of La Chroma, opposite Ragusa, our Richard Cœur-de-Lion suffered his shipwreck, and hither the magistrates of the merchant city passed over to receive the king. For beauty of situation, of architecture, in the picturesque costumes and refined manners of her country population, self-governed Ragusa was distinguished above such of her neighbours as submitted to foreign rule ; her literature and many distinguished citizens earned for her the name of the Slavic Athens ; and from the days of the Serbian Czars down to her own subjection to the yoke of Austria, her merchants frequented all marts between the Adriatic and the Bosphorus. Should the lands between the Danube and the Adriatic ever be united under a national government, and Ragusa be connected by railway with Belgrade, it might rise to the position of a winter capital ; it is now the residence of an ancient and genuine South Slavonic aristocracy, once patricians of the republic. Some families are descendants of those that left the inland country when it was overrun by the Turks, and there are instances of a great house having one branch Catholic nobles of Ragusa, and another Mussulman Beys in the Herzegovina.* Austria, with traditional jealousy of Slavonic development, does all she can to divest Ragusa of importance, and to efface it before its northern neighbour Spalato, just as, from her jealousy of Italian development, she seeks to efface Venice before Trieste. We do not go on to speak of the cities of Dalmatia, because, from their accessible situation, they have already been fre-

---

pire, where, perhaps, as much money has been raised for roads as in the most civilised countries, but where I scarcely ever saw a road worthy the name, excepting one for the Sultan's evening drive, and one made by a French company between Beyrout and Damascus.—H. S.

* One of their most distinguished and public-spirited members told us that the Slav aristocracy had properly none but *official* titles, and that the titles now borne at Ragusa were of foreign origin. We may add, as a sign of the times, that formerly in Ragusa many Slavonic names were Italianised, whereas at present, families of Italian origin are found writing their names *Slavicè*. An interesting article on Serb titles, official dignities, and the first and second orders of nobility (vlastelin, vlastelichich) is to be found in the Serbian dictionary of Danichich. Montesquieu observes of Ragusa, " A Raguse le chef de la république change tous les mois ; les autres officiers, toutes les semaines ; le gouverneur du château, tous les jours. Ceci ne peut avoir lieu que dans une petite république environnée de puissances formidables qui corrompraient aisément de petits magistrats."--'De l'Esprit des Lois.'

quently described; also because, except Ragusa, their civilisation is Italian, and obtained under foreign rule. Herein they especially differ from Serbia, where whatever is is of home-growth, and where no language but the Slavonic has ever been in use. The Slavs themselves are fond of saying that Dalmatia stands to Serbia in the relation in which some years ago the more refined and artistic populations of Italy stood to rough little Piedmont — the nucleus of self-government and self-defence.

Another marked Slavonic city is *Agram*—Slav. *Zagreb*—capital of Croatia. It is divided into an ecclesiastical and a secular town, the latter bearing the name of the Fortress, the former of the " Chapter," and containing a handsome cathedral. As an inland town, Agram has no considerable trade; but it forms the focus of such South Slavonic patriotism and literature as are to be found in the Latin Church. The Croats are carrying on negotiations with Vienna, to get back that self-government which they stipulated to retain when their crown was placed on the head of a Hapsburg. They are also endeavouring to reinstate Slavonic instead of Latin services throughout their churches. These efforts give a colour too local and political for general interest to most of the literary productions of Agram; but as honourable exceptions may be instanced, some epic poems which display an objective simplicity of style, a natural vigour of sentiment and detail, favourably contrasting with the unreal and sensuous tone of German poetry of the present day.

In Slavonia, the little town of *Diakova* is remarkable as containing the seminary of the Roman Catholic clergy for Bosnia. Until lately its members were dispersed for education to convents in Italy and elsewhere, and thus were trained to religious fanaticism, while they lost national *esprit de corps*. At Diakova they are carefully instructed in their own language, and prompted to co-operate with Christians of every denomination against the common enemies—barbarism and Islam.

Fiume—Slav. *Rieka*—a port on the Adriatic, geographically belongs to Croatia, but was assigned by Maria Theresa to Hungary. It still remains a bone of contention between Hungarians and Croats to the benefit of their mutual enemy, the Austrian Government, which at the time of our visit had saddled the town with a preposterous garrison. The railway already alluded to would unite Fiume with Agram, Sissek, Semlin, Belgrade, and other towns on the Danube and Save.

South of Austrian Croatia lies Turkish Croatia, and south again of that the Turkish province of Bosnia. The chief place of Bosnia is *Bosna Seraï*, or *Saraïevo*, as the people call it—a

town of from forty to fifty thousand inhabitants, built on
both sides of a small river, and finely placed among woods
and hills. The beautiful situation of Saraïevo procured it the
name of "Western Damascus," and as the only large city in
that part of Turkey, marvellous stories were told of the number of its mosques and the splendour of its bazaars. For long,
although so near to Europe, it was almost inaccessible to
Frankish travellers; nor would the proud Slavonic Mussulmans, descendants of a Christian nobility, tolerate the presence of a Turkish governor within the walls of their Seraï.
But since the trampling of Bosnia by Omer Pasha, Saraïevo
has become less unattainable, and lost much of its prestige,
besides that from its situation it is growing every day less important as a place of trade. It is now the residence of a Turkish
Vezir and European Consuls, and of the richest Mussulman
landholders and Christian merchants who yet remain in the
western provinces of Turkey in Europe.*

Mostar—Slav. *Stari Most* (old bridge)—capital of the Herzegovina (or Duchy of St Sava), is a wretched town, with nothing
to recommend it save its beautiful bridge, built before the Turkish
conquest.

Prizren and *Ipek* are the principal towns of Stara or Old
Serbia, a district intervening between the principality of Serbia
and the north of Macedonia. Prizren still shows the ruins
of churches, erected while it was the capital of the Serbian
empire and seat of a great yearly fair. Ipek is interesting
as the site of the ancient Serbian patriarchate, of which the
church still remains. The beautiful church of Dechani, built of
three kinds of marble, and best preserved of all Serbian monu-
ments, lies between Ipek and Prizren. The country around used
to be church-land, and is described in ancient documents as thick-
set with monasteries and villages, and traversed by numerous commercial roads. Under the rule of the Turk it has become almost
a desert.

Nish, Sophia, Philipopolis, Skopia, Prilip, Tirnova, Vidin,
Shumla, Shistova, are the principal towns of Bulgaria. In them
are to be found such Turks as inhabit, and, as it were, garrison
the province, the country people being almost exclusively Christian. Tirnova was the ancient Bulgarian capital. We were not
allowed to go thither, on excuse that the neighbourhood was in

* Osman Pasha, who was Vezir of Bosnia at the time of our journey, is considered one of the best-natured governors in Turkey, and really seemed to do
all that was possible under the circumstances. The British Consul, Mr Holmes,
is an accomplished draughtsman, and in his beautiful sketches has done full
justice to the scenery of Saraïevo.

commotion, and we were afterwards told that there, under the shadow of the Balkan, the Christians are bolder and more enterprising than elsewhere. *Ochrida,** once the seat of the Bulgarian Patriarch, is celebrated for its lake scenery, and preserves an ancient church.

Salonica,† Thessalonica—*Slav.* Solun—the port of southern Bulgaria, and surrounded by a Bulgarian population, does not contain more than 500 Bulgarian families. Of its 60,000 citizens, a large proportion are Hebrews, who are also the richest and most considered.‡ The Turkish Government permits them to have a printing-press, an indulgence hitherto denied to the Greeks; and almost everything they think desirable can be got out of the Pasha by bribes. *Salonica* yields at present the curious instance of a city historically Greek, politically Turkish, geographically Bulgarian, ethnographically Jewish.

Last among the places of importance in the South Slavonic countries we must mention the most important of all—*Belgrade.* Situated at the junction of two large rivers, and forming the natural terminus of railroads uniting four seas, Belgrade is evidently declared by nature, if not, as has been said, the capital of a south-eastern empire, at least the capital of the South Slavonic lands.

The history of war between Austria, Hungary, and the Ottoman, tells how often Belgrade has changed masters, becoming by turns the rampart of Western civilisation and the prison-gate of Turkish barbarism. Neither the gallant kingdom of Hungary nor the powerful empire of Germany could retain for Christendom the key of the East; it was won by a rising of peasants, who, entering on the struggle with no weapons but their

* Finlay says, Samuel (King of Bulgaria at the end of the tenth century) "established the central administration of his dominions at Achrida. . . . . To Achrida he transferred the Bulgarian patriarchate. . . . As a military position Achrida had many advantages: it commanded an important point in the Via Egnatia, the great commercial road connecting the Adriatic with Bulgaria, as well as with Thessalonica and Constantinople. The site was also well adapted for rapid communications with his Slavonic subjects in Macedonia, who furnished his armies with their best recruits."—'History of the Byzantine Empire,' p. 438.

† "The admirable situation of Thessalonica, and the fertility of the surrounding country, watered by several noble rivers, still enables it to nourish a population of upwards of sixty thousand souls. Nature has made it the capital and seaport of a rich and extensive district, and under a good government it could not fail to become one of the largest and most flourishing cities on the shores of the Mediterranean."—'History of the Byzantine Empire,' Finlay, p. 317.

‡ The number of the Jews at Salonica is estimated at 40,000, but with their usual astuteness they contrive to avoid being taxed individually, and the community bribes the Turkish officials to let them pass without scrutiny for no more than 11,500.

staves, ended it with arms taken from the enemy. The city of
Belgrade is now in possession of the Serbian people, and for a
time they even gained its fortress; but by the treaty in which the
Porte agreed to recognise the autonomy of Serbia it stipulated
to retain certain stations on the Danube, and among the rest
the Castle of Belgrade. We have already alluded to the inconveniences of this arrangement—inconveniences which the presence of a Mohammedan garrison would inflict on any Christian
city, but trebled when that city is a *port*.

The Principality of Serbia is smaller than Scotland, and with
little more than a million of inhabitants; it is true their numbers are rapidly increasing, but none are wealthy, and within a
generation they were Turkish rayahs. It is needless to say
that under such circumstances Serbia has not much to export,
and hence it has been argued that Turkish cannon at Belgrade
do not really check its commerce, because it has no commerce
to check.

We would answer that the position of Belgrade marks it as
the port of regions far wider than the Principality of Serbia.
Once let the vast countries behind it be opened to European
intercourse, and Belgrade itself declared a free port, and there is
scarce a bound to the extension of its trade—always supposing
that within its walls the merchant is not exposed to have his
warehouse set on fire and his head carried off his shoulders by a
Turkish bomb. The Serbs have as yet had no opportunity of
developing commercial industry; but to have an idea of what
they might do if unchecked by hostile influences, let us see
what they have done in other ways where that influence could
not interfere. Compare the state and number of roads in Serbia
with those in Bosnia, Bulgaria, nay, in Greece. Compare the
general security of life and property, and the peremptory re-
pression of brigandage whenever it shows itself, with the unpunished lawlessness that disgraces Greece and Turkey, and the
prevalence of robbery even in the adjacent provinces of Austria.

Above all, look at the progress of education among a people
which, at the time of its liberation, was composed of swineherds
and tillers of the soil. Little more than thirty years ago there
was not in Serbia a single school—now there are schools in
every village, gymnasia in the principal towns, in Belgrade a
theological seminary and two academies.

Speaking only from personal experience, of places where we
have lived, and persons and things that we have seen, we
should say that, notwithstanding many faults and shortcomings, the contrast presented by the Serbians to cognate
populations under rule of Turkey, and the progress made by

Serbia since she has been suffered to govern herself, give fair ground for belief that increase of political liberty would be well bestowed on the South Slavonic race—that is to say, that with this race freedom would not degenerate into anarchy, nor break its bounds in revolution. Not but what there is at present real danger of revolution in that part of the world, but it lies in the provinces misgoverned by Turkey, of which the exasperated populations will certainly not stick at trifles should they see an opportunity of breaking the yoke. Wherever the Mussulman stands to the Christian in the place of an oppressive privileged landholder, and the Christian to the Mussulman in that of a crushed villein, there we must expect that the first stage of emancipation will be *massacre*. Already the trodden are looking forward soon to avenge the wrongs of centuries, and the threatened are preparing to sell their lives dear. Suppose an outbreak to occur in Bosnia—and a spark may kindle it any day—we must have forgotten the story of Syria if we can believe that either the power or the will to avert slaughter will be found with the Government of the Porte. And if not there, where shall we seek it? What foreign interference is to check bloodshed and restore order? or rather, while it is yet time, let us inquire what change of system might avert the crisis which impends over the Slavonic provinces of Turkey, by giving to the Christian his lawful position, instead of waiting till he seizes it as he may?

Austria is ready with an expedient. She says, " Give at least Bosnia and Herzegovina to me, and see if I do not keep them quiet." Doubtless as quiet as Hungary or Venice, and at the same cost ; for not even Venetians or Hungarians hate Austria as do all classes, all creeds, in these coveted Slavonic lands.* Besides, if Austria is to have one bit of Turkey, Russia will claim

---

* It has more than once been mooted that the Slavonic provinces of Turkey might with advantage be merged in Austria, an empire great part of whose subjects belong to the Slavonic race. But these people have a national proverb, " The Slav is one thing, the German another." They look upon themselves as members of a great race, with a great future before it ; whereas the Austrian Government is of opinion that a little perseverance on its part will metamorphose Slavs, Magyars, and Roumans into Germans, and that the future is to belong to the Germans and the Germanised. Hence the non-German peoples under Austria are ever struggling against injustice, and the Southern Slavs have no desire to enter the same boat with them ; they even declare it better to suffer Turkish barbarism, with an ultimate prospect of deliverance, than to share Austrian quasi-civilisation at the price of losing their only hope of national Slavonic existence. The Austrians have also a happy knack of making themselves so much disliked, that in Turkey Christians declare they would join arms with Mohammedans, and Mohammedans with Christians, to prevent the whitecoats crossing the border. Even if they were made over to her, Austria could never hold these countries except by force, and the inhabitants would implore Russia to assist them against her, so that this arrangement would hardly be favourable to the future peace of eastern Europe.

another. The Eastern question is booming in our ears—the dismemberment of the Ottoman Empire has begun.

But may not guardians more eligible, because more natural, be found for the malcontent Serbian subjects of Turkey in their own kinsfolk of the Principality? Serbia herself presents an instance of a Slavonic province of the Ottoman Empire acquiring self-government without the empire being dismembered, without falling into anarchy, without becoming the prey of any foreign power. Suppose the government of the Principality were intrusted to organise and educate another million or so of Serbians, and in return required to pay a respectable tribute *—thus for years to come would its energies find legitimate occupation — thus would the Christians, now subject to foreign and destested rule, be *gradually trained* to govern themselves.† With respect to Bosnia, it may be objected that to impose on it a Christian governor would rouse the Mussulmans to fanatical fury. Once this was true, but of late years the Beys have seen their power and riches pass from them to officials from Constantinople; they dread to lose their all by a Christian insurrection, and would gladly make terms while they may. Their national antipathy to the Osmanlis is much on a par with their religious antipathy to the Ghiaour, and they certainly would be glad to exchange the necessity of bribing a needy and greedy pasha for the hope of being patronised by a prince of independent fortune, and characterised by munificence, equity, and good faith.

To the question, whether even the strongest considerations of self-interest would ever induce Slavonic Mussulmans to coalesce with Christians of the same race? the answer must be sought in the recent behaviour of those Mussulmans themselves. The

---

* It is said that the tribute of Serbia to the Porte does not defray the cost of the single fortress of Belgrade, and that altogether the Sultan spends, on keeping down his western provinces, more than he derives from them in revenue.

† We give this suggestion because we heard it in the country itself, and because its tone is somewhat more practical than the countless expedients of outsiders. Ubicini says :—

"La Serbie est le point de mer, le kiblè, comme disent les Arabes, de ces populations, qui, en proie à des malaises divers, aspirent à échapper à leurs dominateurs actuels. C'est chez elle que se réfugient, comme dans un lieu d'asile, les raïas opprimés de la vieille Serbie et de la Bosnie, les révoltés de l'Herzegovine, les Albanias persécutés, les Bulgares nécessiteux. Les Serbes d'Autriche, ballottés sans cesse entre Vienne et Pesth, se tournent vers Belgrade, et regardent le Prince Michael comme le chef et le protecteur natural de leur race."—' Revue des Deux Mondes,' Mai 1864.

This is literally true; for besides the immigrants among the lower orders, the Senate and Ministry of Serbia include persons born in the Slavonic provinces subject to Turkey and Austria. Many of these—and, among others, one who is a native of Bosnia—have relatives residing beyond the border. As for Bulgaria, when, some years ago, political changes were expected, a deputation from thence offered the post of ruler to Michael Obrenovitch, now Prince of Serbia.

Bosniac chiefs, who revolted some years ago, certainly called on the Christians to make common cause against the Ottomans, and some even went the length of putting arms into the rayahs' hands. Again, those Mohammedans who were lately obliged to evacuate the towns of Serbia, made it no secret that they would have been glad of the permission of the Porte to accept Prince Michael's terms, and to remain in their homes on condition of living under Christian government. The reason assigned by the latter was very simple, and was not lost on their co-religionists. They said, "The taxes paid in Serbia to the Prince are lighter than those paid in Bosnia to the Sultan."

As for the present relation of the Principality of Serbia to the Ottoman Empire and the possibility of its being made to conduce to the prosperity of both, the subject has been lately discussed in an interesting article in the 'Quarterly Review.' Therein it is remarked that, at least at present, dependence on the Porte is safer for Serbia than an independence abandoned to the aggressions of her northern neighbours; allusion is also made to a period when the ruler of Serbia was the Sultan's ally and friend. We can attest that all this is admitted by the Serbs themselves, especially by the more practical and experienced, who keep the danger of being overrun by Austrian soldiers continually before their eyes. But their admissions are coupled with important qualifications. They remark that in the days when Serbia was the Sultan's ally she was a *whole* Serbia, not that mutilated fraction now alone known by the name; also that in those days the conditions of vassalage were limited to tribute, with a certain amount of assistance in time of war. They admit that it is reasonable for a small country, if secure of autonomy, and in consideration of practical advantages, to be willing to recognise a foreign suzerain; but they declare that Serbia must risk everything rather than acquiesce in the presence of Mohammedan soldiery, or renounce the prospect of seeing Christian self-government gradually extended to all the Slavonic provinces of Turkey.*

---

* On the question of restoring self-government to Slavonic nations south of the Danube, we may quote Mr Finlay:—

"The entrance of Russia into the political system of the European nations was marked by an attempt to take Constantinople, a project which it has often revived, and which the progress of civilisation seems to indicate must now be realised at no very distant date, unless the revival of the Bulgarian kingdom to the south of the Danube create a new Slavonian power in the east of Europe capable of arresting its progress."— 'The Byzantine Empire,' Finlay, p. 223.

The following note we owe to a member of Parliament well acquainted with the East :—

It is most remarkable that, while England has encouraged almost all nationa movements for self-government throughout Europe, she should throw every

On the subject of this and all other aspirations of the Christian dependencies of the Porte, it may not be out of place to observe that there exists an hypothesis which in the minds of many persons outweighs every other view of the Eastern question. It is assumed that any diminution of the authority of the Turk in any part of the Ottoman Empire must necessarily be attended by a corresponding accession of power and influence to Russia. We would submit that this hypothesis, on whatever grounds it may rest, is hardly supported by the facts of recent history. Since the commencement of this century various parts of the Sultan's dominions have emancipated themselves from Turkish government. Not to speak of Egypt, Roumania and Serbia have achieved autonomy, and part of Greece has been erected into a separate kingdom. In no one of these cases has the loosening of connection with the Ottoman Empire resulted in annexation to Russia, nor even in an increase of Russian influence. Impatience of foreign dictation has grown with the sentiment of independent nationality, and the small rising states of eastern Europe have sought to escape the undue influence of one great Power by securing the favour and assistance of its rivals. Greece has courted British protection in a fashion too obvious to be ignored, and even in the Danubian Principalities (where Russian patronage is valued in exact proportion to the necessity of counterbalancing Austria or Turkey) unmistakable efforts have been made to conciliate the Western Powers. Both Roumania and Serbia in their recent difficulties turned for justice and sympathy to France, and were met with every encouragement; in spite of every discouragement, they still turn to England. Judging, then, from what has already occurred, one might infer that, at least in Europe, the decay of the Turkish Empire would result in the transfer of its dominions not to any foreign potentate, but to those subject Christian peoples on whose ruins the Ottoman power originally rose. A Greek, a Rouman, and a South Slavonic state would each include the nationality represented by its name, and each would comprise territories equal to some of the most flourishing kingdoms of western Europe.* On the other hand, if, in spite of prophecies

obstacle in the way of even the smallest enlargement of the existing national governments in the Christian provinces of Turkey. Were the principles of autonomy encouraged amongst the various provincial governments already entitled to its use, when the Turks shall have gradually died out of Europe, as they surely will, there would be found a national power strong enough to resist alike the encroachments of Russia, and the self-aggrandising policy of Austria.

* As for Constantinople, the Southern Slavs do not claim it for themselves, but it would not suit them that it should be held either by the Russians or the

and prognostications, Turkey should yet awhile endure, its Danubian dependencies are prepared to respect the tie with their suzerain, stipulating only that their vassalage be exempt from conditions impeding prosperity and development.

Much has been done to content the Roumans by ridding them of the obnoxious Greek monasteries in Wallachia; much might be done to content the Serbians by abolishing the Turkish fortresses on the Danube. Serbia has indeed reason to complain that she is treated more hardly than her sister principalities. Unlike Moldo-Wallachia, her self-government is restricted to a small portion of the population it would naturally include; unlike Moldo-Wallachia, she sees her capital and riverports still shackled by Asiatic garrisons. It is on the latter ground that at present she appeals for an improvement in her position.

 . . . .

We have thus far digressed on the subject of politics, because in that part of the South Slavonic lands which is at present subject to Turkish officials, some change in the system of government is the first thing necessary to the advance of the people and the development of the resources of the country. It is not in the power of England to effect this change by a word; but she can do much to prepare it, and to render the condition of these peoples more tolerable, by extending to them her social and commercial intercourse, and by using in their behalf her preponderating influence with the Porte. Were it only in the political interest of Great Britain, which forbids that these countries fall into the grasp of Russia, one would suggest that they be encouraged to hope for an autonomous national existence rather than be driven to look on Russian government as the alternative from that of Austria or Turkey. But the advantage would not terminate here. It has been nobly said that " no

Greeks. They say that it is a world-capital, and too important to all nations to be the exclusive property of any one; that it should be erected into a free city, with a territory attached, like Hamburg or the old Hanse Towns; and that its neutrality should be guaranteed (as that of the whole of the Ottoman dominions is at present) by a compact of the European Powers. The idea that the empire of the Turks in Europe and in Asia must pass *entire* to some other governing race is abhorrent to both Roumans and Slavs, who accuse the Greeks of propagating this doctrine as a means of securing dominion over the other Christians. They ask why the lands that once formed the Eastern Roman Empire should not be divided under separate monarchies, like the lands that formed the Western Roman Empire; they ask if the wide realms of Russia and Austria are more civilised or even more powerful than France, or if their inhabitants are freer and happier than those of Holland, Belgium, and Switzerland. They cannot find in history that an extraordinary extent of territorial dominion has ever been favourable to self-defence, much less to the development of liberty and of culture.

European people can pass from misfortune to prosperity without all European peoples profiting by the change." The countries that we have endeavoured to describe in the preceding pages are not likely to prove an exception to the rule.

The South Slavonic lands are rich in minerals, in forests, and in fertile plains; they have extensive seaboard and navigable rivers; they are peopled by primitive and hardy races, whose spirit of nationality and tenacity of existence have outlived five centuries of crushing and struggle: surely such countries might furnish their neighbours with something more profitable than puzzles for diplomatists or pretexts for war.

NOTE.

THE map of roads is given as evincing the progress made in this respect by Serbia as compared with either Turkey or Greece.

The speech of the Prince strikes us as deserving notice for the picture it gives of the actual state of his little country, and for its freedom from that magniloquent style cultivated in Bucharest, Constantinople, and elsewhere, but especially for the frankness with which it exposes shortcomings and sore points. The reference to the suzerain power is conceived in moderate and respectful terms, but it is distinctly stated that a continuance of friendly relations can only be secured by the consent of the Porte to abandon claims from which it derives no advantage, and which are to the Serbs an impediment to commercial prosperity, and a wound to national self-respect. The last paragraph of the speech refers to the means adopted to stifle a conspiracy of certain interested persons to upset the Government, and thus give the unfriendly neighbours of Serbia a pretext for interference. The Prince's mildness caused it to be presumed that he would allow himself to be unseated rather than resort to exceptional measures; and when he defeated these calculations, the same persons who had ridiculed his supposed leniency were open-mouthed to cry out on him as a tyrant.

Whether, in maintaining his place at the head of the Government, the Prince acts in conformity with the will of the people, may be judged from the following facts:—Some years ago Prince Alexander Karageorgevitch, knowing of plots to unseat him, dared not to face a National Assembly; and when at length obliged to summon it, was at once deposed,

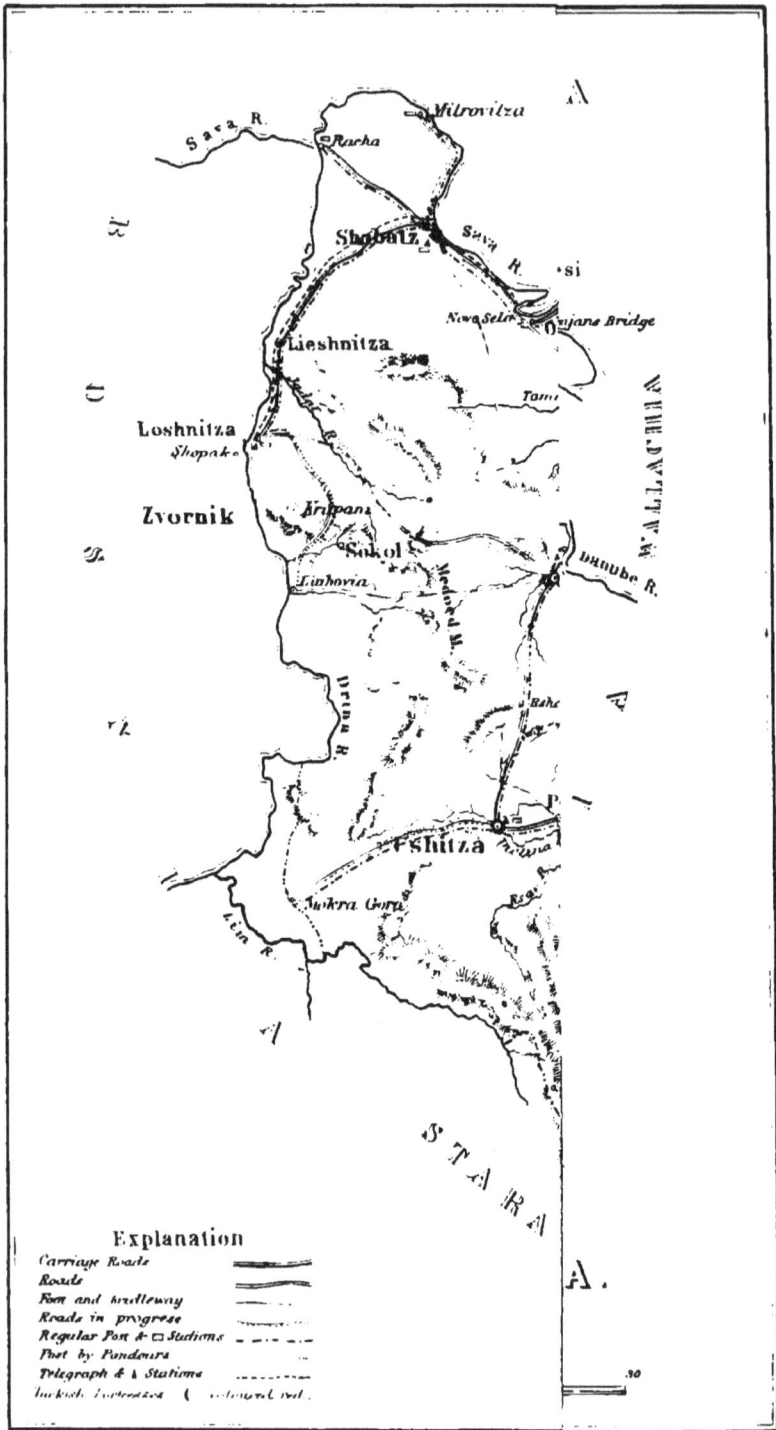

Mitrovitza

Sara R.

Racha

Shabatz

Sava R.

·si

Nova Selo

Danjane Bridge

Lieshnitza

Tam

Loshnitza

Shopake

Zvornik

Kripani

Sokol

Linhovia

Medved M.

Danube R.

Drina R.

Bah

P.

Ushitza

Mokra Gora

Reg

Lim R.

S T A R A.

A.

W. & A. K. Johnston, Edinburgh.

and driven from the land. Prince Michael Obrenovitch summons his Skoupshtina punctually, and holds it, not, as usual, in the centre of the country, but at Belgrade, within view of Turkish and Austrian fortresses, and in presence of the diplomatic agents of foreign Powers.

Under such circumstances, and among a people which keeps the military force of the country in its own hands, it must have been beyond Prince Michael's power to repress the exhibition of an inimical sentiment, supposing such to have existed in the popular mind. The Skoupshtina received him with more than usual heartiness, and voted absolute confidence in his government and policy.

DISCOURS
prononcé à l'occasion de l'Ouverture de
l'Assemblée Nationale,
par S. A. S. le Prince Régnant de Serbie,
à Belgrade, le 16 Août 1864.

(Traduction.)

CHERS REPRÉSENTANTS DU PEUPLE,—

Je suis heureux de me trouver de nouveau au milieu de vous, car la réunion des représentants de la nation autour de moi est pour mon gouvernement la meilleure occasion de s'éclairer avec le concours du pays sur son état et sur ses besoins, afin que, fort de l'appui de la nation, il puisse continuer avec de nouvelles forces ses travaux pour le bonheur de notre chère patrie.

Depuis la clôture de la dernière assemblée nationale, nous avons eu de difficiles épreuves à traverser ; notre patrie frappée d'une profonde émotion par le bombardement de notre capitale, s'est trouvée à la veille d'événements dont il était impossible de prévoir les conséquences. L'intervention des puissances garantes prévint le renouvellement des conflits ; puis intervint entre la S. Porte et les puissances garantes un accord, lequel, comme je le disais dans ma proclamation du 24 Septembre 1862, sans répondre complètement à notre attente, n'en a pas moins amené la réalisation de ceux de nos droits restés jusqu'alors lettre morte. De plus, et grâce à cette entente de nouvelles garanties et de nouveaux avantages ont été acquis à la Serbie.

Toutes les dispositions arrêtées dans la conférence de Constantinople n'ont pas reçu encore leur éxécution. Les Turcs qui habitaient autour des forteresses de Belgrade, de Chabatz, d'Oujitsa, et de Sokol, ont il est vrai quitté leurs demeures, et les fortifications de Sokol et d'Oujitsa ont été rasées ; mais il reste encore à faire évacuer la population musulmane du Petit-

Zvornik et de Sakhar, comme à faire disparaître le castel qui, par sa position au bord du Danube offre un double obstacle aux communications. La question relative au rayon de la forteresse de Belgrade attend toujours sa solution, et la commission mixte à laquelle incombe la fixation des indemnités à accorder au Musulmans pour leurs propriétés abandonées, n'est pas encore arrivée au terme de son travail. Je n'ai cependant cessé de travailler à ce que les decisions de la Conférence de Constantinople fussent exécutées en tout point et le plus tôt possible. Je compte sur la bienveillance et l'équité de la S. Porte pour que ces dispositions aient leur plein accomplissement.

Il est fort naturel que les graves événements que je viens de rappeler aient dû compromettre nos relations avec la puissance suzeraine, toutefois je suis heureux de pouvoir vous assurer que ces rapports sont en voie de constante amélioration. Je m'efforcerai autant qu'il est en moi de favoriser cette amélioration, car j'en attends d'heureuses conséquences pour nos intérêts réciproques. A mon grand regret, la situation anormale et précaire dans laquelle nous maintiennent les forteresses rend très-difficile le succès d'une bonne politique. Néanmoins, en comparant le fâcheux effet des forteresses avec les avantages qui pourraient résulter d'un autre état de choses, je crois pouvoir espérer que la S. Porte arrivera à cette conviction, que la Serbie satisfaite et rassurée serait pour l'Empire un boulevard beaucoup plus fort que les forteresses qu'elle possède sur nos frontières. La vérité se fraie toujours son chemin, et elle le fera ici, je l'espère d'autant plus rapidement, qu'elle a à faire appel à la haute sagesse du suzerain de la Serbie.

Ce n'est qu'avec reconnaissance que je puis vous parler des dispositions des Puissances garantes envers moi et la Serbie. Les témoignages de bienveillance et de sympathie qui nous viennent de leur part sont pour moi une sûre garantie que leur appui ne nous fera pas défaut dans nos légitimes aspirations.

La prospérité de la patrie est restée le but constant de mes efforts ; le développement moral et matériel du pays, toutes les branches de l'administration, la vie du peuple sous toutes ses faces, ont été l'objet de ma sérieuse sollicitude. De nouvelles lois et de nouveaux réglements ont été sanctionnés, dans lesquels nous avons toujours eu en vue d'assurer la stabilité au progrès, et au pays le règne de l'ordre et de la légalité ; car telle est la seule base sur laquelle on puisse asseoir le bien-être d'un peuple. Mais naturellement on ne peut porter de jugement équitable et complet sur les ordonnances émanées du Gouvernement, qu'en tenant compte de toutes les circonstances comme de toutes les raisons qui ne peuvent trouver place dans ces lois, et qu'autant qu'on est à même d'apprécier les intérêts graves et lointains que tout gouvernement doit avoir constamment devant les yeux. Mes ministres vous exposeront en plus grand détail ce qui a été fait dans ce sens durant les trois dernières années. Leurs explications vous convaincront que nous n'avons point perdu de vue les résolutions de la dernière assemblée nationale, mais qu'au contraire nous en avons tenu compte autant que les circonstances nous l'ont permis.

Au nombre des préoccupations du Gouvernement, qui ont pour but d'introduire partout les améliorations nécessaires, j'ai à mentionner une meilleure organisation communale. Vous serez consultés sur ce sujet après avoir été plus exactement renseignés. La position de la Commune est d'une haute importance dans l'Etat, aussi le secours de votre expérience est-il nécessaire au Gouvernement avant que d'entreprendre cette réorganisation.

La question des chemins de fer dont je me promets de très-grands avantages pour le pays, nous occupe depuis quelque temps. Plusieurs offres nous ont été faites à cet égard par des compagnies étrangères et dès que cette importante question aura été suffisamment étudiée on ne manquera pas de faire tout ce qu'exigent les intérêts du pays.

J'ai été bien péniblement affecté des malheurs où les inondations du printemps ont plongé un grand nombre de familles. Mais d'un côté les mesures prises par le Gouvernement jointes aux secours particuliers, et de l'autre l'activité des populations et une année fertile auront, je l'espère, pour résultat de soulager la misère où elles sont tombées et de permettre de réparer promptement les pertes essuyées.

C'est avec joie que j'ai observé combien le peuple pendant ces dernières années s'est plus appliqué au travail que par le passé, de telle sorte que malgré la sécheresse de ces deux dernières années, les chiffres d'exportation n'ont jamais été aussi élevés. Je désire que le peuple ne se ralentisse jamais dans son zèle au travail et veillerai à ce que rien de ce qui peut l'aider et l'encourager dans cette voie ne soit négligé de la part de mon gouvernement. Cette activité jointe aux bienfaisants effets de la "Direction des Fonds," instituée en 1862, a eu pour résultat, Dieu soit loué, de relever la population de l'état d'obération dans lequel elle était tombée.

Il m'est pénible de quitter ces sujets sur lesquels on aime à s'arrêter, pour en aborder un autre très-peu satisfaisant. Nos forêts qui sont pour le pays une grande source de richesse se détruisent sans merci. J'éprouve une vive jouissance à me trouver toutes les fois que je le puis, dans notre beau pays au milieu de la nation, mais l'aspect de ces forêts dévastées me remplit chaque fois de tristesse. Il m'est difficile de comprendre comment l'on ne s'aperçoit pas qu'on tarit ainsi une source abondante de richesse et qu'on détruit une chose qui rend au pays de grands bienfaits. Ne croyez pas que la destruction des forêts ne soit pas à un haut degré la cause des infortunes que les inondations nous font déplorer cette année. Il est temps enfin de porter remède à ce mal. La postérité nous maudira si nous ne prenons soin de lui conserver des richesses que nous ne tenons pas de notre travail, mais que nos pères nous ont transmises. Mes Ministres ont l'ordre exprès de consulter l'assemblée nationale sur les mesures à prendre pour la conservation des forêts et le reboisement des parties dévastées.

Le nouveau système d'impôt n'a pu être introduit. Mon Gouvernement a rencontré des difficultés qui l'ont arrêté dans son application. De cette manière nous nous trouvons encore régis par l'ancien système, système aussi inique qu'insuffisant, et sous lequel il est impossible de rester plus longtemps. Car si, d'un côté il est de notre devoir de faire cesser l'iniquité d'un impôt qui fait trop peu de distinction entre le riche et le pauvre dans le support des charges de l'Etat, de l'autre côté notre devoir est également de procurer á l'Etat les moyens nécessaires pour faire face aux exigences et s'acquitter de son mandat. Vous serez exactement renseignés sur l'état de cette affaire et consultés aussi bien sur le mode d'augmenter les revenus de l'Etat, que sur l'introduction d'un système d'impôt juste et rationnel. Je recommande ces questions à votre patriotisme et à votre équité.

Dans le but d'accroître les revenus de l'Etat, un double impôt a été établi cette année sur le tabac et sur le sel. Ces impôts sont tout-à-fait conformes á l'équité et répondent aux exigences économiques, car ils ne pèsent que sur le consommateur et en raison directe de la consommation, aussi la charge en est-elle peu sensible. A côté de ces avantages son recouvrement n'occasionne ni frais ni peine.

Trois ans se sont écoulés depuis que fut décrétée la création d'une milice nationale, et je puis vous dire que nous possédons déjà une armée nationale organisée. Je remercie la nation de l'empressement qu'elle a mis à me seconder pour arriver si promptement à ce beau résultat. De mon côte j'ai tâché et je tâcherai que notre milice nationale, tout en restant dans les meilleures conditions soit toujours le moins onéreuse possible pour le peuple. Toutefois nous ne devons pas oublier à cette occasion que rien ne se crée sans effort.

Divers projets nous ont été prêtés lors de l'organisation de notre milice nationale ; or cette milice existe déjà et cependant chacun a pu se convaincre jusqu'à présent qu'elle n'est un danger pour personne, mais uniquement la sauvegarde de l'ordre et de la légalité.

La sécurité dont nous avons eu lieu de nous glorifier a été troublée dans quelques arrondissements par le développement du brigandage. Cette circonstance nous a obligés d'augmenter la sévérité des lois et de constituer dans quelques départements un état de choses extraordinaire. Ces mesures ont eu un excellent résultat en ramenant la sécurité et en faisant cesser dans ces contrées l'inquiétude qu'y faisaient règner les malfaiteurs. Il m'est agréable de mentionner ici les services que la milice nationale a déjà rendus au pays dans cette occasion.

Vous comprendrez aisément combien j'ai dû être douloureusement affecté, lorsqu'au milieu de la tâche que je me suis imposée de relever la Serbie et de la conduire dans la voie du progrès ; j'ai rencontré les menées de quelques-uns de ses enfants, qui, entreprenant de me créer des difficultés et de diviser notre force naissante et partant encore faible, se sont oubliés au point de fomenter un véritable bouleversement dans le pays. Mais, quelle que soit la tristesse que ce fait lui-même m'ait causée, j'ai été encore plus peiné qu'il se soit trouvé chez nous un tribunal, et qui plus est un premier tribunal, qui pût couvrir de sa protection de pareils hommes et les laisser sans punition en dépit de la clarté des lois. Il m'a été pénible de faire ce à quoi m'a contraint le procédé inouï du grand tribunal. Toutefois je n'ai pu hésiter un moment à remplir un devoir sacré. Notre premier devoir en effet envers le pays est de le préserver de l'anarchie, et s'il n'est pas ponctuellement rempli tout le reste en vain.

J'espère voir dans peu de temps commencer pour la Serbie une ère de bonheur où nous ne nous souviendrons de faits pareils que comme d'un passé regrettable effacé sans retour. Tous mes efforts tendront à ce but.

Votre amour de la patrie et les preuves d'attachement que vous m'avez données jusqu'à présent, sont pour moi une solide garantie que vous resterez constamment à mes côtés, et que vous me seconderez puissamment dans la prompte réalisation de mon désir le plus cher, qui est de voir la Serbie en possession de la paix et du bien-être, marcher d'un pas assuré vers son avenir. C'est seulement en agissant de cette manière que nous remplirons consciencieusement notre devoir ici-bas et que nous parviendrons à élever un édifice éternellement durable, puis que nous pourrons, quand les temps seront venus rendre un compte irréprochable de nos œuvres devant le Juge Suprême.

L'assemblée nationale est ouverte. Que Dieu bénisse la Serbie et que vos travaux soient heureux !

The answer of the Skoupshtina makes so incongruous an appearance in its French translation, that it would do it injustice to quote from it at length. It commends the Prince for his paternal care of the country, likening him to a wise house-father, and it professes that the people will be willing to intrust him with more of their money, having acquired the conviction that in his hands it is safe to be expended only for the interest of the community.

The notice of the Turkish fortresses so strongly marks a feeling to which we have had occasion to allude that we give it here as it stands:—

ADDRESSE

présentée au nom de l'Assemblée Nationale
à S. A. S. le Prince Régnant de Serbie,
Belgrade, le 20 Août 1864.

(*Traduction.*)

. . . .

Réunie pour la première fois depuis les pénibles circonstances où le bombardement de la ville de Belgrade avait plongé notre patrie, l'Assemblée Nationale saisit cette occasion d'assurer à Votre Altesse que, si la nation serbe a accepté telles quelles les décisions de la Conférence de Constantinople, la seule raison en a été que Votre Altesse dans sa sagesse les avait admises. Elle n'en sent pas moins pourtant avec Votre Altesse, que toutes ses légitimes espérances n'ont pas été réalisées.

L'Assemblée Nationale a vu d'après le discours du trône que nos relations

E

avec la cour suzeraine se sont améliorées. Mais Votre Altesse Sérénissime ne sera pas surprise d'entendre que nous souffrons de voir les Turcs demeurer encore à Sakhar et au Petit-Zvornik, ainsi que de voir les communications entre la Serbie orientale et le Haut-Danube gênées par une forteresse turque qui peut à chaque instant intercepter le passage. Enfin, ce qui nous contriste le plus, est de voir même après le bombardement de Belgrade, les canons des forteresses turques braqués sur les plus importantes de nos villes. Prince, tout progrès réel est interdit à la Serbie aussi longtemps que ces forteresses entretiendront le pays dans de continuelles appréhensions. Les habitants de la Serbie ne pourront se rassurer tant que, sous ce rapport aussi, satisfaction ne sera pas donnée aux réclamations légitimes de Votre Altesse et de toute la nation.

www.ingramcontent.com/pod-product-compliance
Lightning Source LLC
Chambersburg PA
CBHW020249090426
42735CB00010B/1867